EXPLORING

Gulf Islands
National Seashore

Help Us Keep This Guide Up to Date

Every effort has been made by the author and editors to make this guide as accurate and useful as possible. However, many things can change after a guide is published—trails are rerouted, regulations change, techniques evolve, facilities come under new management, etc.

We would love to hear from you concerning your experiences with this guide and how you feel it could be improved and kept up to date. While we may not be able to respond to all comments and suggestions, we'll take them to heart and we'll also make certain to share them with the author. Please send your comments and suggestions to the following address:

The Globe Pequot Press
Reader Response/Editorial Department
P.O. Box 480
Guilford, CT 06437

Or you may e-mail us at:

editorial@globe-pequot.com

Thanks for your input, and happy travels!

A **FALCON** GUIDE®

E X P L O R I N G

Gulf Islands
National Seashore

Robert P. Falls Sr.

FALCON®

GUILFORD, CONNECTICUT
AN IMPRINT OF THE GLOBE PEQUOT PRESS

Front cover photo: Tim Fitzharris/Index Stock Imagery
Back cover photo: Wendell Metzen/Index Stock Imagery
All interior photos by Robert P. Falls Sr.
Maps by Tim Kissell/Trailhead Graphics, Inc., © The Globe Pequot Press

Library of Congress Cataloging-in-Publication Data is available.

ISBN 1-58592-036-3

♻ Text pages printed on recycled paper
Manufactured in the United States of America
First Edition/First Printing

I dedicate this book most lovingly to Jackie,
who never stops believing in me.

"Nature does not like to be anticipated—it too often means death I suppose—but loves to surprise; in fact seems to justify itself to man in that way, restoring his youth to him each time—the true fountain of youth."

Walter Inglis Anderson

CONTENTS

Acknowledgments

Wildlife and nature photography is my passion, and I find that I cannot do it well until I first know the subject thoroughly. Writing is much the same. I consider both to be part of my life's continuing education.

I write to mend that hole in my life that some would call ignorance, and it is a lonely profession, but no one can write a book alone. It requires much input and advice from others, and the list for this undertaking is long. The following are just a few of the special people that shared their time and expertise, to whom I wish to express my heartfelt thanks for contributing to my edification.

Thanks to Park Superintendent Jerry Eubanks and his able crew, all the professionals who are the adhesive that holds together the eleven pieces of this puzzle, and most especially the following:

Gail Bishop, Chief of Interpretation, National Park Service, Gulf Islands National Seashore, Gulf Breeze, Florida. Her thorough knowledge of the facilities and boundless goodwill contributed more than I can possibly say.

Micheal C. Aymond, Park Naturalist, National Park Service, Gulf Islands National Seashore, Gulf Breeze, Florida. The wildflower man at Fort Pickens who, seemingly, has a knowledge of every plant on the planet.

Hank Snyder, Chief of Resource Management, Gulf Islands National Seashore, Gulf Breeze, Florida. He recommends good books.

Gary Hopkins, Resource Management Specialist, National Park Service, Gulf Islands National Seashore, Ocean Springs, Mississippi.

Susan Merrifield, Park Ranger, National Park Service, Gulf Islands National Seashore, Ocean Springs, Mississippi.

Mike Hobbs, Park Ranger, National Park Service, Gulf Islands National Seashore, Ocean Springs, Mississippi.

I also wish to thank Dr. Ervin Otvos, Gulf Coast Research Laboratory, Ocean Springs, Mississippi, who really knows his islands and loves to talk about them.

A grand expression of appreciation goes out to all the wonderful people at the public libraries in Pensacola, Florida; Gulf Breeze, Florida; and Ocean Springs, Mississippi, who assisted in my research. I have come to realize that library employees are intelligent and caring souls, and these people are no exception.

A Special Note from the Author

For more than twenty years, my career as a professional photographer and writer has taken me into many of our national parks in search of nature subjects. I have watched as visitation has increased dramatically, and I am appalled by what these visitors are doing to the facilities.

It is only appropriate that the public visits and enjoys our parks. They were set aside for that purpose, but they were also created to protect the resources, and to a great extent the responsibility for much of that protection rests firmly on the shoulders of the visitors. We must become de facto stewards if our parks are to survive.

The people of the National Park Service do an admirable job, but their resources and personnel are limited, and we, the visiting public, must accept some of the load. To that end I have written this field guide with the sincere hope that readers will realize what a very special place is this Gulf Islands National Seashore and will treat the park with the respect it deserves.

At the end of each chapter I have included some "Photo Tips," which I hope will aid the visitor in capturing their park memories on film. So see and enjoy, experience these beautiful islands, these historic structures, but please do not abuse the facilities, which are supported by *our* tax dollars.

Introduction

■ Gulf Islands National Seashore

Snow-white crystalline sand, sparkling azure-colored waters, and world-class fishing are but three of the attractions that draw sun worshippers to the beaches of the Gulf Coast. But when they tire of these pursuits, visitors can find numerous other natural wonders to peak their interest, and nowhere are they more plentiful than at the Gulf Islands National Seashore (GINS). A unit of the National Park Service, the GINS includes some of the barrier islands that lie along the Florida and Mississippi coasts in a humid, hot-temperate climate zone.

The largest of ten national seashores, GINS encompasses approximately 139,775 acres; that number being approximate because the size of the barrier islands is constantly changing. Nationally, the East Coast is home to the largest concentration of national seashores at seven, with two on the Gulf Coast and one on the Pacific Coast. Cape Hatteras, on the coast of North Carolina, was the first so designated, but it did not become a reality until 1953. The various seashore units were not developed under a single plan, such as that of the Wild and Scenic Rivers Act, for instance. Through specific legislation each is protected by its own charter and is managed by the National Park Service.

Over the twenty-two years following the Cape Hatteras designation, all ten parks were created through the dedicated efforts of environmentally minded individuals who would see at least part of their favorite coastline

1

protected from mindless development. In four of the parks, Fire Island, Cumberland Island, Point Reyes, and Gulf Islands, that protection has extended to the establishment of wilderness areas.

Unfortunately this individuality means all national seashores are not managed the same. Some have bowed to pressure to allow off-road vehicles on their beaches. In these places the destructive power of these machines has irreparably damaged the resources. Gulf Islands is not one of these; all motorized vehicles of any type are banned from the beaches.

The Gulf Islands National Seashore was created in 1971 through the joint efforts of concerned citizens on the coasts of two states. Florida residents, who were attempting to save the old historic forts in the Pensacola area, joined forces with Mississippi residents, who had marshaled an effort to preserve Fort Massachusetts on Ship Island. Their alliance made it possible to persuade a reticent U.S. Congress that this proposed park was a worthy cause, and the protection of the barrier islands also was included in the mandate.

The details of the difficulties encountered on the road to the park's creation could fill a book in their own right. The story goes back to the 1930s when the NPS expressed interest in establishing a national monument on Ship Island but was stymied by the U.S. Public Health Service, which still operated a quarantine station on the island.

During the forties and fifties, local developers envisioned a resort community on Santa Rosa Island that would bring large-scale tourism to Pensacola, and supporters of park development in the Pensacola area were pushed into the background. Only Fort Pickens received any attention, being established as a state historical park in 1949.

Not until the mid-1960s, after two decades of unplanned commercial development on the island, would the park movement surface again, and supporters still faced a six-year battle before the park was created. Political wrangling and infighting stood in the way. Citizen groups for and against the park struggled, and predictors of doom foretold of the "federal land grab" that would develop. Many of those involved—primarily commercial land developers—favored a "local solution," park development by the state. At various times certain sections of federally held land were even transferred to state control, but these plans never succeeded either.

In 1966 the NPS released an ambitious proposal for the park that would include all the present properties plus Cat Island; Ono Island, off the coast of Alabama; and the Chandeleur Islands, near Louisiana. But these would not be included, for various reasons, when the final proposal was put before Congress and approved in 1971.

■ Understanding Barrier Islands

Webster's Dictionary defines the word *fragile* as: "barely able to endure, without harm, the normal day-to-day physical demands of existence." Fragile aptly describes most barrier islands, which are very special places, and the islands in this group are no exception. In *The Edges of the Sea,* the renowned naturalist Rachel Carson once wrote about sand beaches: "They are infinitely variable, each grain on a beach is the result of processes that go back into the shadowy beginnings of life, or of the Earth itself."

Basically barrier islands are just large piles of sand created by the power of the sea, appearing to be permanent, but in fact continuously changing— a work in progress. Barrier islands buffer the mainland from storms and create an environment of shelter for abundant plant and animal species on the islands themselves, in the sound behind, and in the bayous on the mainland.

The Gulf Islands National Seashore encompasses several of these fascinating islands, stretching from West Ship Island near Biloxi, Mississippi, to the eastern end of Santa Rosa Island near Destin, Florida—a distance of 150 miles. This is no park in the ordinary sense of the word; it is fragmented into eleven different units, spread across the coasts of two states.

After Gulf Islands National Seashore was established in 1971, being recognized as the last undisturbed islands in a chain stretching from Maine to Texas, Congress acted in 1978 to set aside Horn Island and Petit Bois Island as wilderness areas. The concept of islands as designated wilderness can, perhaps, be better explained by the following passages excerpted from the National Wilderness Act of 1964: "An area where the Earth and its community of life are untrammeled by man, where man himself is a visitor and does not remain." A wilderness area must retain "its primeval character and influence without permanent improvements or human habitation." And "it must generally appear to have been affected primarily by the forces of nature, with the imprint of man's work substantially unnoticeable."

Sea oats on beach, Destin, Florida.

At the end of the last "ice age," known as the Pleistocene epoch, retreat-ing glacial ice in the Appalachian Mountains crushed and ground huge boulders and bedrock into sand, and the basic ingredient of the barrier islands was born. On the eastern face of the mountains, snowmelt and rain carried the sand to the Atlantic shores. On the western slopes, it flowed toward the Gulf of Mexico.

Some barrier islands are formed when a sandy peninsula extending sea-ward from the mainland is breached by a storm, but rarely does this type last very long. Others are thought to form when an existing high ground along the shoreline is surrounded by the rising sea level and gradually widens seaward to form a viable island. The sea islands of the Atlantic Coast are examples of this second construction method, but scientists who have studied the Gulf islands see a different mode of origin.

Composed of fine quartz sand eroded from the Appalachian Mountains and borne to the coast by rivers that feed the region, such as the Choctawhatchee and Appalachicola, the islands were constructed by wind and wave action and occurred where a special set of circumstances existed. In the words of Dr. Ervin Otvos, of the Gulf Coast Marine Research Laboratory in Ocean Springs, Mississippi, "In areas of gently sloping near-shore bottoms with adequate sand supply, shoaling waves construct under-water platforms of sand over the mud bottoms, upon which the islands form through aggradation." They are known as microtidal barriers, because the coastline has a tidal range of less than six feet, and the islands tend to be quite exaggerated in length compared with their width.

Despite earlier theories that island sand was deposited during high storm tides, Otvos holds to the theory that island building—at least in this area—"occurs during fair weather periods of constructive waves, sometimes with sustained high sea levels. . . . Permanent establishment of the present large Mississippi barrier islands may have taken many years or even cen-turies after conditions first became favorable in the area for island forma-tion." Otvos estimates they began emerging some 2,500 to 3,500 years ago.

These islands tend to grow toward the west; longshore movement of waves wears away the eastern ends and builds up the western ends in a barely perceptible but continuous process that also widens the island.

The barrier island environment is composed of several zones: the beach waterline, foredunes, swale, backdune, then possibly a forested barrier flat and/or a salt marsh. The foredune line, or primary dunes, are the first-line defenses from storms and will usually be the highest in elevation. Behind that the interdunal swale is actually a temporary wetland, holding water for a short time, following a rain or flooding, which is stabilized by low-growth xeric plants, such as pennywort and sea oats. The backdune line will be farther inland, and then the barrier flat that may, or may not, be maritime forest, a very important element of the island stabilization process, likely consisting of slash pine and sand live oaks. By far the most critical element of the barrier complex is the beach, which must bear the brunt of the high-energy surf. The inland coast of the island may consist of shallow shoals and salt marsh due to the low wave energy. These communities of nonwoody, salt-tolerant plants, consisting primarily of black needlerush and smooth cordgrass, occur at the interface of sand and water.

Salt marshes are highly productive, exhibiting characteristics of both terrestrial and marine ecosystems, featuring many fascinating animals that are abundant but not widely diverse. Residents of the marsh must be capable of withstanding extremes in temperature and high concentrations of salt. A good example is the fascinating fiddler crab, which can be observed at low tide when it is most active, feeding on the detritus of the grasses. Fiddler crabs are actually aquatic organisms and must carry respiratory water in their gills. Because it is also used for evaporative cooling and to enhance the crab's feeding process, the water must be frequently replenished. To that end the crabs bore hundreds of burrows down to below the water table, passing through the root system of the plants, a process that has proven beneficial to the production of the marsh grasses.

Terrestrial visitors include raccoons, marsh rabbits, and rats and mice, while sparrows, wrens, clapper rails, and various wading birds, such as herons and egrets, are typical avian guests. Add a myriad of small fishes, shrimp, mussels, oysters, and other species of crabs and it becomes apparent that these areas, which at first glance appear desolate, are actually teeming with life.

Like most coastal environments, barrier islands are affected by global warming. As polar ice caps melt, ocean levels continue to rise. Conservative estimates for the year 2100 are for ocean levels from four to seven feet above today's levels. How rising sea levels will affect the barrier islands is a matter of conjecture at this point and depends on available sediment to compensate for it and the frequency of hurricanes, which interrupts calm-weather island growth. The best guess is that these islands will not migrate toward the mainland as shorelines move inland but will continue to rise rather than be drowned by the rising water.

Relentless winds, both onshore and offshore, cause small-scale shifting of sands, prevented only by vegetation, including the venerable sea oat, which has a complex root system extending deep into the dune. Sea oats and dunes exist in a symbiotic relationship, as one grows, so does the other, and when a storm flattens one of the islands, sea oats are planted to renew the dune-building process. Their relevance has prompted the NPS to post warnings in all public facilities and in all publications about not picking the plants.

Twisted and gnarled, trees grow in bizarre and often grotesque configurations in this environment as their roots fail to find sufficient purchase in the loose sands to allow them to grow straight and tall. Some that gave up the struggle long ago remain as mere skeletons, bleached and scoured by the elements to the color of polished pewter. Several species of the southern pine are often found alongside the live oak, but they do not fare as well for they are much softer woods.

It takes very little to disrupt the geological or ecological balance of the islands, and they have a turbulent history. In the eighteenth century a hurricane severed the western tip of Dauphin Island, near the coast of Alabama, and this spit of land subsequently migrated 8 miles to the west to become Petit Bois (Little Wood) Island in Mississippi.

At the turn of the last century, a resort and gambling casino named Isle of Caprice was constructed on Dog Key, midway between present-day Horn and Ship Islands. Casino owners had a sweet operation until left with only a submerged sandbar. More recently the horrendous Hurricane Camille cut Ship Island into two parts in 1969.

Throughout this book you'll see the word *hurricane* mentioned frequently. Even the earliest accounts of Gulf Coast exploration mention these terrifying storms. They have shaped and reshaped the barrier islands for centuries, totally annihilating some and impacting early efforts to colonize the area.

More recently, Hurricane Erin raked across Santa Rosa Island near Pensacola (August 1995). Opal came right behind it in October 1995, making landfall within a few miles of Erin's location, inflicting heavy damage in the Navarre area. Such are the forces affecting barrier islands, and today's residents of the Gulf Coast accept such storms as a way of life.

In their delicate natural balance, undeveloped barrier islands preserve a rich variety of wildlife. According to the National Park Service, more than 250 species of birds have been identified on the islands, which provide nesting areas for plovers, ospreys, and others. Many wading birds, including herons and egrets, roam the shallow flats in search of food, and gulls float effortlessly on the ever-present wind currents as if suspended by an invisible wire, providing excellent photo opportunities. Less human intrusion means less intimidation for the wildlife, and in the "off seasons" these wild creatures are much easier to approach. In spring and fall numerous migratory birds can be found on the islands, including the endangered peregrine falcon; the stunning hooded merganser duck winters in the area. An alligator might even be found sunning itself along the banks of a bayou.

Mammal populations are scarce, but they do include raccoons, rabbits, otters, and nutria. A red wolf nursery program was conducted on Horn Island for several years during the nineties to determine if this endangered specie could procreate in such a harsh environment. The experiment was successful and they have since been withdrawn. Bald eagles that were reintroduced by the U.S. Fish and Wildlife Service have begun nesting in the islands. Hopefully they will once again become a permanent part of the delicate ecological balance.

Natural diversity is a large segment of the park's attractions, offering numerous vignettes of nature in a rapidly developing suburban environment, but natural history is not the only consideration. The GINS also encompasses areas on the mainland of Florida and Mississippi where cultural history is at the center of interest.

Over the centuries the intrusion of humankind came from many quarters. French, Spanish, and English explorers built settlements and forts in the Pensacola Bay area as early as the 1500s, and later a young United States government would build coastal fortifications, some of which have been restored and opened to the public. The different flags that have flown over the area are a patchwork quilt of conflict, and the struggles of three great powers sound very much like children squabbling over a shiny toy. A modicum of local history is necessary for a complete understanding of how all eleven park units are interrelated.

Native Americans were, of course, the first inhabitants, and archaeological traces of their presence can still be found at the Naval Live Oaks unit out-

Sport fishing boat, Destin, Florida.

side Pensacola. Nomadic bands of Paleo-Indians wandered these shores after the last ice age, 9,000 to 7,000 B.C. They were hunter-gatherers who moved their camps in relation to the herds of large wild animals they hunted. In lean times they fished with hooks made of bone and hand hewn-stone.

During the Archaic period, 6,000 to 2,000 B.C., Indians supplemented their diets with more fish and plant food while some agricultural practices developed. Toward the end of this period the art of pottery for cooking was developed.

During the Deptford period, 1,000 B.C. to A.D. 1, the natives lived in coastal villages but traveled inland to gather fruits, nuts, and berries. The Santa Rosa Swift-Creek period and the Weeden Island periods followed; changes in pottery delineated the different cultures. Permanent villages were established and the dead were interred in burial mounds along with ornaments and pottery.

The last pre-European periods were those of the Pensacola and Fort Walton peoples, including the Panzacola Indians, from whose name was dervied "Pensacola." Some moved farther inland for the better agricultural opportunities, some remained at the coast and were present to greet the first

European explorers to sail into Pensacola Bay.

Reports of the time are sketchy, but it is generally believed that two Spanish explorers, an uncle and nephew named Miruelos, may have been the first to enter Pensacola Bay in 1516. The nephew later sailed with Alonso Alvárez de Pineda to map the northern Gulf Coast and to search for a strait to the East, which they never found.

In 1528 Pánfilo de Narváez landed near Tampa Bay and then continued northward, stopping at several places for supplies. Many years later a relic discovered near Pensacola indicated that it had been one of his stops. These explorations would result in the fabled expedition of Hernando de Soto in 1539. De Soto landed at Tampa and proceeded northward on foot. While the main party rested near Appalachee, present day Appalachicola, de Soto sent several parties westward. One, led by Diego Muldonado, entered Pensacola Bay and returned to de Soto with stories of the magnificent bay. Muldonado was sent to Havanna for supplies, and de Soto planned to meet him at Pensacola, but that meeting never materialized as de Soto, instead, moved off northward on other explorations.

Spain's interest in the area waned until rumors of French colonization plans were heard. The perceived need for a sheltered haven for Spanish treasure ships traveling to and from Mexico spurred King Phillip II into action. Don Tristán de Luna y Arellano was well regarded in King Phillip's court, a veteran of thirty years service, and possessed a family fortune. He was a logical choice for governor of Florida and was chosen to colonize the area.

Don Tristán and his expedition of 1,000 civilians and 500 soldiers, on thirteen ships sailed into Pensacola Bay on August 14, 1559, after a grueling, stormy voyage of sixty-three days, during which part of their supplies were lost. Luna named the bay Santa Maria Filipina in honor of his king, the first of many names that would be imposed on the area.

The exact location of his landing is unknown, but from his description, it is believed to be on the high bluff near present day Fort Barrancas. Luna set about his duties immediately. Two parties of colonists were sent inland in search of friendly Indians and food. Their remaining supplies stayed aboard ships until suitable protective structures could be erected.

Five days after landing on August 19, Luna received his second bad experience with unpredictable Gulf Coast weather. A vicious hurricane entered the bay and rained havoc down upon the group for twenty-four hours. When the weather cleared, Luna was left with only three ships, and his expedition had experienced a significant loss of lives and supplies. One of the surviving ships was sent to New Spain, in Mexico, for help and supplies, but it never came because the food situation there and in Cuba was also critical.

Don Tristán experienced the first of a number of illnesses as he dealt with starving, demoralized, and almost mutinous troops. Some colonists advocated moving the settlement inland where crops could be raised. Luna was hesitant, thinking that relief would surely come, and many left without him. When Don Tristán's long-awaited relief ships finally arrived, the supplies were meager, and he decided to send the sick and noncombatants back to New Spain.

One year after the first landing, only 360 of the original 1,500 people remained, and they refused to obey Luna. The viceroy at New Spain sent a new governor to replace him, but the settlement was finally abandoned, and when Luna died in Spain, he was still blamed for the failure of the Pensacola settlement. Had it survived, Pensacola would have been the oldest city in Florida instead of St. Augustine, which was founded in 1565.

European interest in the area waned and was not revived for 125 years. In the late seventeenth century, England and France again expressed interest, and Spain, wishing to protect its shipping interests and hearing rumors of a French colony in the area, sent out eleven different expeditions to find the elusive French. Only the ruins of the La Salle settlement at Matagorda Bay (on the Texas coast) were ever found. But one of the Spanish expedition leaders, Juan Enriques Barroto sailed into Pensacola Bay in February 1686, and this time the discovery sparked an international race for its possession. Admiral Andres de Pez was commissioned by the King of Spain and sailed into the bay on April 7, 1693, promptly giving it a new name: Bahia de Santa María de Galve. A member of the party, a geographer named Dr. Carlos de Sigüenza y Góngora, was the first person to map the bay and its shores, naming the prominent sites. He saved the point of Santa Rosa Island at the mouth of the bay for himself, calling it Sigüenza Point. Sigüenza penned glowing reports of the bay, but Spanish interest still languished. Not until 1698, when Britain and France readied ships to explore Gulf waters, did Spain order an expedition to occupy Pensacola Bay immediately. Three ships requisitioned supplies and set sail, landing at Barranca de Santo Tome (the present site of Fort Barrancas) on November 21 with 300 infantrymen and a battalion of laborers. Within six days temporary quarters were built and construction of Pensacola's first fort had begun. When finished, Fort San Carlos de Austria had eighteen cannon peering out to sea to discourage any invaders who might wander into the bay.

Unknown to the Spaniards, the French were also exploring the Gulf Coast, but farther to the west. The French were more interested in colonizing the territory around the mouth of the Mississippi River, and Pierre Le Moyne d'Iberville's exploration of the barrier islands led him to use Ship Island as his base of operations while establishing the French settlement at New Orleans.

By 1700 Pensacola's weather and the shifting sands had rendered the Spanish fort practically useless. Despite vigorous recruitment of colonists in New Spain, the settlement's population had dwindled to 212 by 1712.

Supported by the British, who had also become interested in the area, Creek Indians attacked the fort on several occasions and burned some of the buildings, sapping the strength of the garrison, a condition that the French would soon exploit.

In 1718 England signed a treaty with Austria and Holland and declared war on Spain. France followed suit in 1719, and, on May 14 surprised the Spaniards when a fleet of French ships appeared off Santa Rosa Island. Cannon fire was exchanged, and when the French captured the dunes above the fort, Governor Matamoras promptly surrendered. The French settled a garrison of 250 souls at Fort San Carlos, raised the French colors up the flagpole, and called the area Pensacolle. But their victory would be short lived. The Spaniards captured two French ships and used them as decoys to recapture the fort, then sat about strengthening the fortifications.

The French again sailed into the bay in September 1719 and recaptured the fort. This time they burned the village and blew up the fort. Nothing remained of the original settlement. When peace was established in 1720, Pensacola was returned to the Spanish through negotiation, and they were faced with beginning anew. Reconstruction of the settlement began and a fort was constructed on the point at Santa Rosa Island. It was also the beginning of a new community, but storms and high tides continually ravaged the village. In 1752 a hurricane left only two buildings standing, and the people returned to the mainland.

In 1763, at the end of the Seven Years War, the Spaniards once again sailed away from Pensacola, having ceded all their holdings in Florida to the British, who promptly divided it into the provinces of East and West Florida, with Pensacola as capital of West Florida.

When commanding officer Major William Forbes sailed into Pensacola, he called it a dismal sight. Perhaps he knew nothing of the hurricanes that had devastated Spanish-held Pensacola. Civilian settlement of the village was encouraged by land grants from the crown. British colonizer Elias Durnford was ordered to create a plan for the city and the fort and barracks. Some of his original design can still be seen today in the Seville Square Historic District of Pensacola. The city failed to prosper, and beginning in 1764, a series of new governors of West Florida were installed without success. The colony was in near chaos when Peter Chester was installed as governor in 1770. An able administrator, he restored order and some progress was seen. But dark clouds were gathering to the west.

Bernardo de Gálvez, Spanish governor of Louisiana, was delighted when Spain entered the American Revolution in 1779—as an ally of France, not America—for he was well prepared to attack the British at Pensacola. After capturing settlements along the Mississippi River, he breached the walls and captured the English-held fort at Mobile. Then Gálvez recruited forces from Havana and turned his sights toward Pensacola.

On the morning of March 8, 1781, he appeared at the mouth of the bay with sixty-four ships and a force of 1,300 soldiers, some of which he landed on Santa Rosa Island. The remaining troops were landed at Barrancas, where they were joined by 1,400 troops from New Orleans and 900 from Mobile. Gálvez and his soldiers encircled Fort George, which had been constructed at Gage Hill north of the city, and launched a two-day siege. When a lucky cannon shot exploded the munitions storage at the fort, it was surrendered to him and the Spanish flag once again flew over Pensacola.

Most of the English departed under the change of flags, but a few remained and built successful businesses. The Spaniards retained the British plan for the city but changed the street names to reflect their Spanish heritage, and many of those names survive today in the modern city. Settlers came from the Caribbean Islands. Food was raised in local gardens, and trade with the Creek Indians brought beef for a growing population. Two sawmills were constructed on the Escambia River, and other businesses fol-

Dwarfed magnolia tree in bloom, Pensacola, Florida.

lowed. The city flourished, but Andrew Jackson, who was by then well entrenched as an American military leader, had other plans for Pensacola.

Several events conspired to pique Jackson's interest in West Florida. The Louisiana Purchase of 1803 gave the United States most of the territory west of the Perdido River, and during a Creek Indian uprising in 1813 500 Americans at Fort Mims, north of Mobile, were massacred. When word reached Jackson that Creek Indians paraded 250 scalps from Fort Mims before the Spaniards in the streets of Pensacola, he led his Tennessee forces against the Creeks at Horseshoe Bend, and defeated them. Some Indian survivors fled to Pensacola, where the British merchants aided them. Jackson sent an ultimatum to the governor of Pensacola who promptly expelled the British, who then began support of the Indians in the Apalachiacola area. So in 1818, Jackson marched on Pensacola, seething in anger for the British and the Indians. He captured the city and Fort Barrancas, shipped prisoners off to Cuba, and installed an American governor.

The Spanish government complained of Jackson's high-handed actions and entered into negotiations with the United States for the Floridas. The

Adams-Onis treaty was finally signed in 1819, and by 1821 Pensacola was an American possession. Andrew Jackson was the obvious choice for governor and was commissioned by President James Monroe. A mayor and city council was authorized and a court system established. American settlers arrived in large numbers. Cotton from Alabama and Mississippi flowed through the port, and lumber became an important business. The city thrived and prospered. In 1821 Jackson notified the President that he had completed organizing the government of Florida and returned to his Hermitage Plantation in Tennessee.

Construction of the navy yard began in 1825, and Pensacola entered into a long and beneficial relationship with the U.S. Navy. A plan had been formulated by Navy Secretary Samuel L. Southard for a naval live oak reservation to provide the wood so prized in shipbuilding. In 1828 he purchased the first tract of 1,300 acres, and it eventually grew to approximately 150,000 acres, 90,000 of which were in the Florida territory. This was the first—and only—such enterprise because wooden ships became obsolete during the Civil War when ironclads were introduced.

The Army also came to the area, and in the 1830s, Captain William H. Chase of the U.S. Army Corps of Engineers was appointed to build a series of coastal fortifications to protect the city and the Navy Yard. Fort Pickens on the western tip of Santa Rosa Island and Fort McRee on the eastern tip of Foster's Island (Perdido Key) were designed to defend the entrance of Pensacola Bay. Fort Barrancas protected the Navy Yard and Advanced Redoubt, .75-mile inland, would protect the inland approach to Barrancas and the Navy Yard. During this same period a decision was made to erect a brick masonry fort on the western end of Ship Island because control of Ship Island Pass was deemed critical to the national defense.

Construction of the forts proceeded slowly due to the lack of materials and skilled labor in the area. Many millions of brick were needed and were originally shipped from Mobile until Chase convinced local businesspeople to establish brick production facilities in Pensacola, which would use clay that was mined north of the city and shipped down the rivers that flow into Pensacola Bay. Another new booming business was thusly created for the area. The amazing growth of the Territory of Florida meant that it was time to apply for statehood, and there was some question as to whether it should be one or two states. Finally, Florida joined the union in 1845.

With statehood the city continued to grow. Even after the forts were completed, the brick industry prospered, shipping most of its product to New Orleans, and lumber emerged as a major industry. Yellow fever decimated the population in the 1850s, but even that could not stop Pensacola. A railroad was under construction that would provide transportation north from the city, and two ships, the U.S.S. *Pensacola* and U.S.S. *Seminole,* were produced at the Navy Yard.

The coming of the Civil War would launch Pensacola into national prominence. Florida was one of the first three states to secede from the Union, even before the Confederate States of America was formed, and both factions wanted control of Pensacola's forts. Lieutenant Adam Slemmer, the commandant at Fort Barrancas, realized his position there was indefensible and quickly moved his troops, supplies, and munitions to Fort Pickens on Santa Rosa Island. From here he could effectively control access to the harbor.

Seven companies of Confederate troops from Alabama and Florida occupied the Navy Yard and Fort Barrancas, and additional Union forces landed at Fort Pickens on the same day that the Confederates fired on Fort Sumter. The Civil War was a reality, and both factions at Pensacola were prepared for battle. In September Union troops secretly scuttled a ship the Confederates were outfitting, and they retaliated with an ill-fated attack on Fort Pickens. Sporadic cannon fire between the forts caused minor damage until a major battle on January 1 and 2, 1862, extensively damaged the Navy Yard and exploded the powder magazine at Fort McRee. Ironically the only action the forts would ever see was not in defense of the harbor, but rather in offensive action against each other.

The Confederate forces were ordered north in February to join the Army of Tennessee after destroying everything useful. Only a token garrison remained, and it surrendered to the U.S. Army on May 10. The citizens of Pensacola fled the city, most of them going to the center of the Confederacy at Montgomery, Alabama, only one hundred or so remained in the city, and weeds grew in the deserted streets. Pensacola was now an occupied city, and Union troops controlled the Navy Yard and Fort Barrancas until Florida adopted a new constitution following the war. Times were hard and money was scarce, but Pensacola would not be held down.

Moonflower in spring, Florida.

During the 1870s Pensacola's railroad became a part of the vast Louisville and Nashville system, allowing access to northern markets. A growing country needed lumber, and the timber business in Pensacola boomed once again. Ships from all over the world docked at the wharves to load lumber, and many Europeans moved to the port city. Pensacola truly became an international city.

The early years of the twentieth century saw a building boom in Pensacola, but timber resources in northern Florida and southern Alabama dwindled, and there were no plans for sustaining them. By 1910 the booming timber business had fizzled. Pensacola's citizens looked to the Navy Yard for support, but "The Yard" had lapsed into obscurity following the Spanish-American War and closed in 1911. Two major banks in the city closed, and Pensacola was trapped in the throes of recession. Fortunately the navy had plans for a naval air training facility and construction began in 1914, providing jobs for the citizenry of nearby Pensacola. Activity at the facility increased markedly with the advent of World War I, and the city became known as the "mother-in-law of the Navy." The Pensacola

Barrier Island coastline on sound, Santa Rosa Island, Florida.

Shipbuilding Company started construction near the city, creating 1,500 jobs. The boomtown was flying again and its dependence on the Navy Yard continued, at least through 1928. And then in 1929 the Great Depression struck Pensacola.

Pensacolians were perhaps more fortunate than the rest of the country. Large construction projects already under way at the naval base kept the city going until they played out in 1931, and then the city plunged into poverty. After that the "make-work" programs of the WPA were all that were available in Pensacola. New streets were built, others repaired, and many of the contracts provided for expansion at the naval air station. That was fortunate for in 1939, as Pensacola fought to recover from the Depression, war erupted in Europe and the base was ready.

The bombing of Pearl Harbor put the naval air station on full alert. The training schedule tripled almost overnight. As the government's involvement in the area increased, the city's economy grew also. The population soared, and it was boom time once again. As the war escalated, units of the army stationed at Fort Barrancas were shipped overseas, and the Naval

School of Photography was moved into the old barracks at Barrancas. The city grew rich from the navy's expansion in the area, but since the end of World War II, Pensacola's economy has grown and diversified so that it is no longer totally dependent on the military.

It has been said that we cannot know where we are going until we know where we have been, and that is the underlying purpose behind any historic preservation. Through boom or bust the forts of the Gulf Islands National Seashore have been involved in the rich history of the area for many decades. It is impossible to find an accounting of that history that does not mention them, and it is only appropriate that they be preserved for the edification of future generations.*

■ For Your Information

At the time of this writing only three of the Florida units at GINS have entry fees: Fort Pickens, Opal Beach on Santa Rosa Island, and Rosamond Beach on Perdido Key. The admission fee buys a seven-day pass that is good at all locations, and annual passes are also available. The National Park Gold Age, Golden Eagle, and Golden Access passes are honored at all fee locations.

Fishing is one of the most popular pastimes for visitors to the Gulf Coast and can be excellent on both the Florida and Mississippi coasts. (More information and details are included in the individual state sections in this guide.)

Whether surf fishing from the beach or a pier, cruising the coast in your own boat, or trying your luck on one of the deep-sea fishing charters, the waters in and around the Gulf Islands National Seashore are bound to offer angling excitement. But be aware that both the states of Florida and Mississippi have different licensing requirements for saltwater and freshwater fishing, and you will want to be current on boating regulations when using your own vessel. A private boat is enjoyable if for no other reason than that you can come and go according to your own schedule. But there are some dangers, and the park rangers at the visitor centers can advise you on the best boating procedures. Pay attention to weather reports when boating in the Gulf, especially during the months of June through November,

Source: Virginia Parks, *Pensacola: Spaniards to Space-Age* (Pensacola Historical Society, Pensacola, 1996).

which is hurricane season in the Gulf of Mexico. Always use personal flotation devices—as prescribed by law—and think twice before drinking alcoholic beverages while boating. Use—and abuse—of alcohol is one of the largest factors involved in deaths on the water; it dehydrates your body in an environment that already calls for drinking more water than usual. *NOTE:* Scuba diving has become quite popular in all areas of the Gulf Coast, and responsible divers use a safety marker buoy with flag. Please be cognizant of such buoys when boating in the area and give the divers a wide berth.

Boat tours to visit Fort Massachusetts on West Ship Island are available out of Gulfport, Mississippi, from spring through early fall, and information on charter boats to the wilderness islands is available at the visitor center in Ocean Springs, Mississippi.

The appropriate agencies to contact are listed in the "For More Information" section at the back of this book. Enjoy your fishing and be safe, and best of luck on bringing that big one back home!

For those with Internet access, the National Park Service has an excellent Web site that will aid in planning your trip: www.nps.gov/guis. The Web site features information on all aspects of visiting the park facilities, including current weather advisories and links to other sites with additional information.

The options afforded by the Gulf Islands National Seashore are many and varied, and whether you begin at the Florida or Mississippi district, your first visit should be at the respective visitor center for information, maps, and directions, so pick your time and pick your island—and remember the sunscreen.

Florida District

Congress established Gulf Islands National Seashore (GINS) in 1971. The purposes of the Park are "to provide recreation for visitors and to protect wildlife, barrier islands, salt marshes, historic structures, and archeological sites along the shores of the Gulf of Mexico." Protected by its own legislation, the park is managed by the National Park Service (NPS), whose extraordinary task it is to protect the resources and accommodate the more than five millions visitors each year.

Barrier islands constitute much of the Park's acreage, and the largest of the Gulf Coast strand of barrier islands by far is Santa Rosa Island. Over the years, much to its detriment, the island has been the subject of considerable and sporadic commercial development. The staggering commercial growth of recent decades has prompted the local chamber of commerce to endow this section of coast with the title of "Miracle Strip," and visitors often refer to the area as the "Redneck Rivera." It does indeed seem out of sync with the rest of the state, and is even located in a different time zone. Eglin Air Force Base controls most of the eastern tip of the island, which has remained undeveloped except for government owned structures that are part of the coastal radar system. Visitors can still see the ocean from the main road. This land is assigned to be part of the GINS at some future date when the military determines that they no longer require its use, and will add significant acreage to the park.

Moving westward, there is a small commercial area across the bridge from the city of Fort Walton Beach. Here are wall-to-wall condominiums and ocean front hotels that partition the sky and obliterate any and all view of the beach. They are hardly ever fully occupied, and still the developers continue to build more.

Once clear of this area, the island is again natural for many miles until the Navarre area, where rental and private waterfront homes predominate. This area has received the brunt of several hurricanes in recent years—two within the same season in 1995—and seems to be in a constant state of rebuilding. Living there must be very like living on the fault line on our nation's West Coast. The average elevation of the island is only 3 to 5 feet above sea level, and storm surge from a Gulf hurricane can easily reach 10 to 12 feet. Many houses are, therefore, built on stilts.

Formation of hurricanes is dependent on three essentials: warm ocean-water (at least 79 degrees), warm humid air, and a source of energy, such as a low-pressure trough. The Gulf provides all three in abundance. Pacific maritime and polar weather fronts from the north and northwest pass through the area almost weekly during fall, winter, and spring. Peak hurricane season is September and October when the ocean temperature is warmest and humidity is highest. In the time that records have been kept, over forty percent of all U.S. hurricanes have made landfall in Florida and most of the early season storms hit the Gulf Coast, as many are formed in the western Caribbean.

Meteorologists name hurricanes as the most destructive type of storm. Although it is true that tornadoes may exhibit higher winds for a short period, the hurricane can often sustain its destructive force for eight to ten days.

A barrier island is not a place to establish a home or business, or any permanent structure for that matter, yet many islands have been heavily built-up on both the Atlantic and Gulf Coasts. Unscrupulous developers are constructing homes in harm's way and those homes are being snapped up by unsuspecting citizens who just want to live by the sea and who are not being informed of the dangers. Development on a barrier island concentrates beach access to far fewer locations and results in an adverse impact to the primary dunes, which occasionally are removed completely, leaving no storm protection.

West of Navarre's stilt houses is one of the largest units of the Gulf Islands National Seashore, a welcome respite from the tackiness of the "Miracle Strip." The stark white sand beach extends for 7½ miles and then is interrupted one last time by the glitter of Pensacola Beach, before ending after 48 miles at the mouth of Pensacola Bay.

Naval Live Oaks ▪ 1

The Naval Live Oaks area is located just across the Santa Rosa Sound from Pensacola Beach. The visitor center also serves as the administrative headquarters for the Gulf Islands National Seashore and is housed in an attractive brick structure beautifully situated in a heavily wooded area. It contains numerous exhibits and offers audiovisual presentations related to the park. A lovely wooden observation deck has been constructed off the rear of the building, extending toward the water. Sunlight filters down through the surrounding pines rising tall and straight, casting shadows across the board floor and providing a refreshing place to sit and plan your day. Other features include a comfort station, a lovely and secluded picnic area, a group camping facility, and several walking trails.

This visitor center celebrates the awesome live oak tree (*Quercus virginiana*) that is so prevalent along the Gulf Coast and often seen heavily draped in Spanish moss. A tree of picturesque proportions, it has a short, thick trunk and broad-spreading crown at maturity. The main branches of the tree can be quite thick and extraordinarily elongated, often extending horizontally and low to the ground. The bark is deeply etched and charcoal colored, and its fruit are acorns that grow up to 1 inch in length. The Florida champion live oak, located near Alachua, is some 340 inches in circumference, 83 feet high, with a 150-foot crown spread!

Long before the turn of the twentieth century, the wood was prized for shipbuilding because of its resistance to disease and decay. The wood is so dense that a single cubic foot can weigh as much as seventy-five pounds,

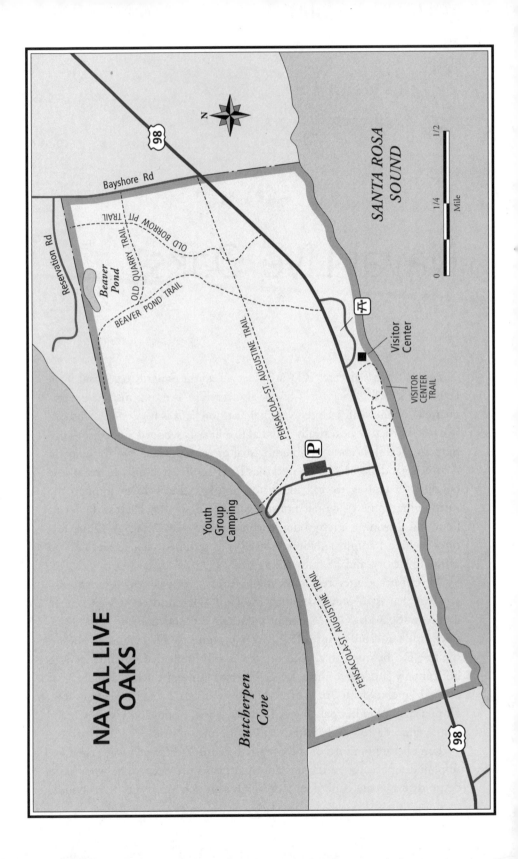

Live oak grove with Spanish moss, Naval Live Oaks area, Gulf Breeze.

compared with about thirty pounds for southern white pine. It was prominently used in the 1700s. The U.S.S. *Constitution*, which is today a National Historic Monument, was assembled of live oak in the 1790s and was nicknamed Old Ironsides during the War of 1812 because of the strength of its construction.

The United States purchased the land in this area in 1828, and President John Quincy Adams authorized the establishment of a tree farm for cultivation of the live oak for naval uses. The wood's prominence would be short lived, however, as the development of ironclad warships late in the nineteenth century made it obsolete. During the restoration of the U.S.S. *Constitution*—from 1927 to 1931—hundreds of tons of naval live oak was shipped to Boston by rail from Pensacola Naval Air Station, where it had been stored underwater since before the Civil War. Some of the same timbers were saved and used for repairs to the ship again in the 1960s, a good indication of its indefectibility. The visitor center features interesting exhibits on this fascinating tree and archeology of the area, covering a long and rich history.

Native Americans lived in the area for at least 10,000 years, and many of the native plants and wildlife provided food and medicine to the peoples of the late Archaic period. Shell middens (refuse piles) found near the water of undeveloped areas such as the national seashore properties are evidence of prehistoric Indian villages dating back as much as 5,000 years. Bones and implements indicate that these hunter-gatherers survived primarily on marine food and native game, such as mammoth and bison, and camped near reliable sources of fresh water, such as the many natural springs.

Stone arrowheads and tools and pottery, artifacts of a later period—around A.D. 700—have been found in the area, indicating that later populations moved more toward agricultural pursuits on the fertile soil of the mainland. It was the extensive cultivation of corn and beans that came to provide sustenance for these native Floridians.

The aboriginal populations changed dramatically in the 1600s as a result of the coming of European explorers who established settlements and introduced Christianity—and disease. Expeditions led by such explorers as Juan Ponce de León, Pánfilo de Narváez, Hernando de Soto, and Don Tristán de Luna y Arellano provide valuable records of contact with native Indian tribes like the Calusa and Apalachee along the Panhandle area. Unfortunately, some two hundred years after the arrival of the first white settlers, indigenous populations of several hundred thousand had been decimated. With immune systems unprepared to cope with the introduced infections, their numbers decreased rapidly, and the few remaining natives were assimilated into European cultures. By the 1740s Creek Indians from what are now Georgia and Alabama established settlements in the area and became known as the Seminoles. The Naval Live Oaks and other units of the national seashore contain some of the last evidence of these early cultures not lost to development, and modern archaeologists still study these sites in an attempt to understand these original residents.

While examining a beach for damage following Hurricane Frederic in 1979, geologist Dr. Jim Morgan made perhaps the most significant find on national seashore property. An intact earthen pot dating back to the Weeden Island period, A.D. 800–A.D. 1,200, was uncovered by shifting sand where it had lain undiscovered for thousands of years. The pot was made of local clay, is a medium brown color, and etched with a checked design. It was in nearly perfect condition, not found in pieces like most of the discoveries made here.

On this site a part of one of Florida's early roads can still be seen. The Pensacola–St. Augustine Mail Road, which was built in 1824, traverses the north side of the Naval Live Oaks property. At present it is only a depression in the soil; a walking trail now partially follows the original route. When exploring this area, please remember that all archeological sites are strictly protected by the National Park Service (NPS) and Federal law prohibits the removal of any historical items.

■ The Trails at Naval Live Oaks

Hiking trails around the 1,378-acre wooded area demonstrate what the forests of Florida might have been like before the first white settlers arrived. Visitors will also see yaupon holly growing wild, accompanied by the ever-present saw palmetto.

The majority of the trails at Naval Live Oaks are located in the wooded parcel of land on the north side of Highway 98, which comprises most of the 1,378 acres at this unit. As you approach the park from either the west or east, you will see continual development right up to the very borders. Every piece of land, no matter how small, has a home or business in place. Such a large parcel of undeveloped land is an oddity on the Florida Gulf Coast, and the unrelenting migration of American citizens to the coastal areas of our continent points out the necessity for protecting such gifts of nature. The National Park Service has been a responsible steward and is to be commended for protecting this valuable habitat.

Although most of the trails are to the north of the highway, you will not want to miss the trail that begins at the visitor center. A free map of all the trails is available at the visitor center, and the NPS has marked the trails with round metal tags that are color coded according to the map legend.

Visitor Center Trail

The Visitor Center Trail begins just off the rear deck at the center and is identified by red-orange markers. It is arranged in a figure eight with a 0.25-mile loop first and a 0.5-mile loop beyond, then extends to the park boundary. The trail leads through mainland forest and has exhibits on native plant life and wildlife. Small signs erected along the pathway depict the various botanical attractions. At the western end of the trail at water's edge is an observation area, where you're likely to find brown pelicans or other seabirds searching for food in the sound. An enchanting grove of the trees for which this unit is named towers above you; the scale is quite humbling.

These live oaks have grown tall in the supportive soil of the mainland. Early Native Americans called such grand trees "standing people," and these fit the description well. The massive limbs stretch outward like misshapen arms, and strands of Spanish moss wave in the gentle breeze like tattered strips of cloth. Here are trees of a configuration to fit well in a Grimm's fairy tale.

Walk among these majestic trees and allow your imagination to soar! You'll almost see elves running along the massive moss-draped limbs and ducking into a protective den at the trunk of the tree. Observe and wonder how big the trees of the virgin forest must have been before humans began "harvesting" them.

The remaining trails are located in the undeveloped, forested land across Highway 98 from the visitor center. Access is from a street that forms the eastern boundary of the park property. For more information please contact the rangers at the visitor center.

Old Quarry Trail

From the visitor center take U.S. Highway 98 east to Bayshore Road and turn north. Go approximately 0.5 mile to the first fire gate on the left. Yellow markers identify the trail that extends a short 0.3 mile to where it intersects with the Old Borrow Pit and Beaver Pond Trails.

Beaver Pond Trail

From the visitor center take U.S. Highway 98 east to Bayshore Road, then north along the eastern boundary of the park. Turn west on Reservation Road, which enters a housing development. Go past the beaver pond, which may be dry, depending on weather conditions, and park on either side of the fire gate, but please *do not* block the fire gate. The 1.0-mile trail is marked by orange tags and extends north to south through large stands of longleaf pine and oak forest, intersecting the Old Quarry Trail and St. Augustine Road Trail, and terminating at Highway 98. Visitors will benefit from keen observation. Wildlife watching can be quite good at the beaver pond. When there's water, blue-gray gnatcatchers feed on insects. Red-winged blackbirds and wading birds, such as herons and egrets, feed among the cordgrass along the water's edge, as marsh rabbits and raccoons sip from the pond's life-giving moisture. An early morning visit will produce best results.

Old Borrow Pit Trail

Access to Old Borrow Pit Trail is through the first fire gate on Reservation Road, before the beaver pond. Walk approximately 0.1 mile to the first trail on the right and look for the red markers. This trail intersects the Old Quarry and Pensacola–St. Augustine Road Trails and extends 0.9 mile through lovely sand pine and longleaf pine communities, terminating at Highway 98. This is second growth forest and of smaller size than that of the Visitor Center Trail, but even in the heat of summer the heavy forest canopy provides shade and a pleasant walking experience. One can easily picture the original Native American residents padding along similar trails in the early days. The undergrowth is thick, and in many places it is trimmed close to the edge of the trail, so that the effect is like walking through a tunnel. Yaupon holly will have beautiful red berries in fall and

This 4,000-year-old pottery was found at Gulf Islands National Seashore.

winter, and in summer look for native red basil plants along all the trails. Rub the leaves between your fingers and sniff the pleasant fragrance. This is natural Florida at its best.

Pensacola–St. Augustine Road Trail

From the visitor center take Highway 98 west to the first road inside the park on the north side of the highway and turn northward. The parking lot is 0.3 mile south of this trail, which runs parallel to Highway 98 for approximately 2.2.miles, roughly following the course of the original road. The environment is a variety of young live oak, pignut hickory, southern magnolia, longleaf pine, and scrub oak. The group camping area, available by reservation, is located inside the locked gate, near the bayside shore. Walk past the gate a short distance to the trailhead on the right and look for blue marker tags. This trail ends at the eastern boundary at Bayshore Road.

As you hike, imagine the horse-drawn wagons of commerce that once plodded along this route or a solitary mounted horseman with a leather dispatch case on his lonely journey of some 400 miles from city to city. You are walking on a piece of history, a path that once spanned what is now the state of Florida, bringing supplies and eagerly awaited mail to the early European settlers.

The trails are open for use during daylight hours. Avid hikers have an adage that fits well here: "Take nothing but photographs, and leave nothing but footprints." Please do not litter or pick wild plants.

Enjoy your visit!

■ Information

ACCESS: From Pensacola follow U.S. Highway 98 across the Pensacola Bay Bridge, through the city of Gulf Breeze, and then eastward a short distance until you see the signs for the Naval Live Oaks area, 1801 Gulf Breeze Parkway, Gulf Breeze, FL 32561; Phone: (850) 934–2600. Open daily: 8:00 A.M. to 5:30 P.M. (central time).

BEST TIME TO VISIT: The busiest season is the summer months, but fall and spring are excellent, even winter can be quite comfortable. The trails will be practically deserted and far more enjoyable. Insect repellant is always a good idea. Special guided tours are conducted throughout the year. Schedules are subject to change so check with the visitor center in advance of your trip.

CAMPING AND LODGING: Camping is available farther east on Highway 98, or at the Fort Pickens area of the GINS just west of Pensacola Beach. The visitor center has directions on all nearby locations. (A shopping center is adjacent to the park's western border, and more shopping is available in Gulf Breeze and across the bay in Pensacola.)

■ Emerald Beach Campground, Highway 98 (1 mile east of Highway 87 junction), Navarre; 77 sites; (850) 939–3431

■ Magnolia Beach Campground, Highway 98 (3.5 miles east of Highway 87 junction), Navarre; 60 sites; (850) 939–2717

■ Navarre Beach Campground, 9201 Navarre Parkway, Navarre; 150 sites; (850) 939–2188

The Blackwater River State Park, to the north of the national seashore, has a small campground, and the surrounding Blackwater River State Forest has several campgrounds located at Bear Lake, Hurricane Lake, Karick Lake, Kruel Lake, and Cold Water. Call (850) 957–4201 for information. Big Lagoon State Recreation Area in Pensacola, west of the Naval Live Oaks area, has a campground with seventy-five sites. Call (850) 492–1595. There are other campgrounds in the Pensacola area but some are for the use of military personnel only. Call ahead for advisory.

There are numerous hotels and motels in Gulf Breeze and across the Santa Rosa Sound at Pensacola Beach:

■ Best Western Inn, 16 Via de Luna Drive, Pensacola Beach; (850) 934–3300

■ Clarion Suites, 20 Via de Luna Drive, Pensacola Beach; (850) 932–4300

■ Hampton Inn, 2 Via de Luna Drive, Pensacola Beach; (850) 932–6800

OTHER INFORMATION: U.S. Highway 98 is an extremely busy thoroughfare with heavy traffic at all hours of the day. Please exercise caution entering or leaving the visitor center, especially if traveling in a motor home or with a large camper-trailer.

All facilities are wheelchair accessible except for the trails, which have a soft sandy surface. A covered picnic pavilion can be reserved by calling (800) 365–2267. A nominal fee is required. Charcoal grills are provided, but open fires are prohibited. Numerous picnic tables are located about the inviting grounds, and a paved walk leads to and along the water's edge. Pets are allowed only if on a leash, but not along beaches or in picnic areas.

This park participates in the Junior Ranger program and six-to-twelve-year-old children can qualify. A handbook and information are available at the visitor center.

All facilities of the Gulf Islands National Seashore in both Florida and Mississippi are located within the central time zone.

A Web site is available at www.nps.gov/guis/ with more information to help you plan your visit.

NEARBY POINTS OF INTEREST:

■ Pensacola's Zoo, which features 700 different species of animals, is located 9.5 miles east of Naval Live Oaks on U.S. Highway 98. Call (850) 932–2229.

■ Pensacola Beach, just across Santa Rosa Sound, features lovely white sand public beaches and abundant shopping and entertainment facilities.

■ Blackwater River State Park, approximately 40 miles north, is part of the award-winning Florida State Park System and is known as the "canoeing capital of Florida." Call (850) 983–5363. Web site: www.dep.state.fl.us/parks.

PHOTO TIPS: Photographing under the shade of the live oaks can be problematic. Light levels will typically be low, even on sunny days, and you may need a tripod for long exposures. Your flash unit will be of little or no use here.

Higher speed film is another option, but larger grain enters the equation, so choose a film based on your own particular needs.

Santa Rosa Island

■ Okaloosa

The easternmost GINS facility is the small Okaloosa unit, located approximately 2 miles east of the Brooks Bridge in Fort Walton Beach. It is wedged in between the Eglin Air Force Base property and the resort row on Highway 98 and is easily missed. Watch for the national seashore sign at the entrance.

This day-use-only unit is on the Choctawhatchee Bay side of the island where the water is calmer, and it provides beach facilities for swimming and sunbathing. Serious sun worshippers who live in the area make use of this facility, and it is also popular with local sailboarding enthusiasts. A small picnic area with limited amenities is nestled among lovely, mature pines that provide pleasant respite from the incessant sun.

Visit the Okaloosa area in spring and see the delicate lavender blooms of conradina, a member of the mint family. This plant is endemic to only a small area of western Florida and is known to some locals as beach heather. It can be found in other areas of the national seashore as well. The blooms attract butterflies, including the striking painted lady, which occasionally visits. Sandwich terns search the shoreline, and laughing gulls issue the familiar call for which they are named. The NPS has provided informational displays, scattered about the park, which tell the story of barrier islands and their natural habitats.

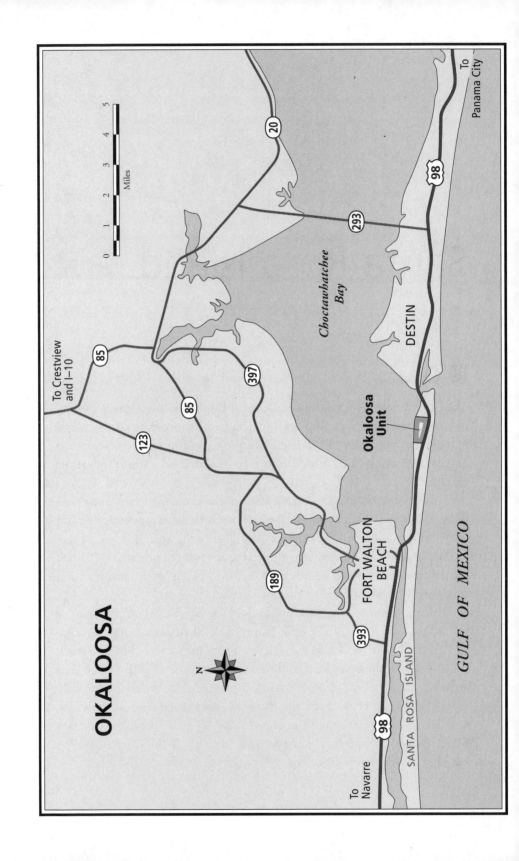

Entrance sign, Santa Rosa Island.

Crabbing and fishing are popular pursuits in the shallow waters. Surf fishing with live bait can be very productive here, but there is no pier available. Possible catches vary according to the season but include trout, drum, sheephead, flounder, and mullet. Nonresident Florida fishing licenses can be purchased for specific numbers of days or by the year. More serious fishing is available a few miles to the east at Destin, which is the home of the largest sport-fishing fleet in Florida. A cobia tournament in March and April awards a $10,000 first prize, and the Destin Rodeo in October is a monster event with over $100,000 in prizes. There is an award for virtually every game fish, and there is no entry fee for anglers fishing aboard boats that are registered in the rodeo. (See the end of this chapter for contact information.)

A boat launch is provided at the far end of the park, but it is not maintained by the NPS, so proceed at your own risk. Better boat facilities are available adjacent to the western boundary at the Leeside Marina (850–243–7359). The Okaloosa unit has no beach facilities on the Gulf side of the island, but Beasley Park, directly across Highway 98, provides beach access and is free to the public.

In summer, sailboats, motorboats, and jet skis can be rented nearby, and parasailing is available. This area is heavily developed, and restaurants and motels are abundant, along with other tourist attractions, in close proximity to the Okaloosa unit.

■ Opal Beach

Farther to the west at Opal Beach, Fort Pickens, or Perdido Key is where the true personality of the Gulf Islands National Seashore reveals itself. A large sign announces the park property as you leave the developed area and enter a different realm. At most places the island is no more than 0.5 mile in width, with the emerald green Gulf of Mexico on one side and the deep blue Santa Rosa Sound on the inland side. Protective coves such as the one at Big Sabine Point offer safe swimming for families with children.

Wading birds stand like silent sentinels at the edge of the water, waiting for some form of prey to wander by within reach of their long daggerlike beaks. Seagulls circle overhead in search of any morsel of food that visitors may drop. All about are rolling sand dunes topped with sea oats that gently sway in the ever-present breeze, and the weathered carcasses of long-dead trees that tried in vain to survive in this spartan environment.

This undeveloped section of island is an important nesting area for beach-dependent wildlife. In recent surveys 18 loggerhead turtle nests have been identified, as well as 300 least tern nests, 15 black skimmer nests, and 58 snowy plover nests. Loggerheads nest on the same beach several times in a season, then may skip two or three years. More than one hundred eggs are laid in an excavated hole and then covered with sand. As many as 70 to 80 percent of the hatchlings will not survive because of predation and a host of other natural threats. Satellite tagging indicates the loggerheads born in northwestern Florida usually stay in the Gulf and will grow to be between 200 and 300 pounds. Unfortunately the nesting season falls between May and the end of October, coinciding with the busiest tourist season at the beach, which infringes on the turtle's nesting habits. Local environmental groups walk the beaches each morning during nesting season and rope off new nest

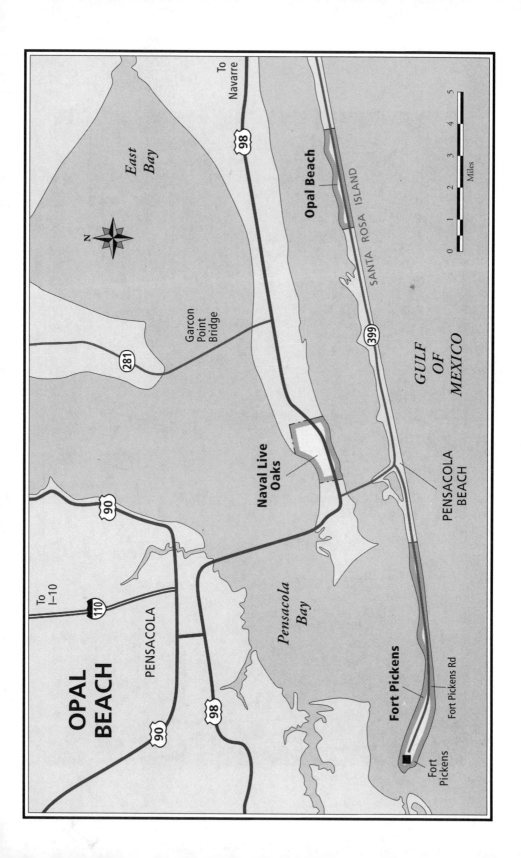

Santa Rosa Island sunset, Fort Walton.

sites in the hope that visitors will not violate them. Loss of habitat and the construction of seawalls on developed islands are other factors blamed for hampering the turtles successful procreation.

Other species found here are the endangered green sea turtles, which are used in turtle soup and suffer from over-fishing, and the snowy plover. Only one hundred breeding pairs of the snowy plover currently exist in the state. They affect a cleaver ruse for predators. This bird will stumble along the sand pretending to have a broken wing to lead predators away from its nest. If you encounter such a demonstration, you are very close to a nest: Please withdraw cautiously. Least and sandwich terns and snowy plovers once nested extensively in the Tampa Bay area but were driven out by development. They now concentrate on the panhandle area where they are once again threatened.

When Hurricane Opal struck this island in 1995, it destroyed 80 percent of the population of the Santa Rosa beach mouse. Surveys done by wildlife biologists since that time indicate enough survived for this white, fur-covered critter to recover and continue its role in the preservation of the sand dunes. The mice on this island face another threat, however, coming from the developed areas. Cats from nearby homes, which are allowed to roam unfettered, feed on the mice.

Wildflower admirers will enjoy a visit also. Yes, there are wildflowers at the beach! Beginning in spring, various species bloom through the summer and into autumn. Flat marshy areas between the dunes, called swales, will be covered in yellow-eyed grass, and pennywort is common, occasionally covered in the golden orange vine of dodder. Swamp coreopsis intermingled with butterfly pea adds an occasional flash of yellow color, as beach morning glory crawls across the sand, opening its lovely white blooms to the morning sky. The variety of such plants will be a pleasant surprise. Look closely, another splash of subtle color is provided by the newly emerging sea oat sprouts of spring. Their diminutive blades, extending only two or three inches above the surface of the sand, are softly bathed in mauve and teal. The heavily developed areas of southern Florida have a problem with introduced, exotic plants that take over and squeeze out natural plants. The panhandle area has fewer introduced plants, and Santa Rosa Island is one of the largest areas of *natural* plant life in the entire state.

This unspoiled parcel of coastal beauty has a timeless feeling, which offers a pleasant change from the continuous development of surrounding areas. State Highway 399, which is the only access, meanders along the beachfront in what can only be described as a captivating drive. But to properly appreciate the area, you must abandon the automobile and wander along the beach, observing the endless dunes shouldered against a limitless sky.

Please heed any signs erected by the National Park Service, otherwise you may walk into a wild bird nesting area or a dune restoration area and destroy the efforts to maintain nature, as it was meant to be. The beaches here feature the whitest sand of any Florida beach and contrast greatly with the water's color, which will be its most attractive at low tide. In shallow water the white sand of the bottom reflects light back up through the water, giving it a resonance unparalleled on other coastlines. Tidal charts can be obtained at the Pensacola Beach Visitor Center or at local convenience stores, and are broadcast on local television news programs.

Inside the park borders, Highway 399 is posted with NO PARKING ALONG ROADSIDE signs, and those who choose to ignore the regulation will likely get stuck in the soft sand shoulder and even more likely be cited by a park ranger. Off-road parking is allowed at the Opal Beach facilities and at three more, smaller, beach access points. Look for boardwalks that cross over the dunes to protect the plants.

The Opal Beach area is another day-use facility located midway along the beach, providing picnic facilities, bathrooms, and exterior showers for swimmers. These facilities replace the ones destroyed by the hurricanes of 1995 and are relatively new, having been completed in early 2000. Elevated boardwalks cross the delicate dunes for beach-goers, and information kiosks detail the NPS's efforts to restore and maintain the fragile quality of this environment. There is no food service available for many miles in either direction so bring food with you for a picnic or cookout.

If you are a good angler, perhaps you can catch your meal in the Gulf. No pier is provided, but surf fishing is allowed, and no permit from the NPS is needed. However, appropriate salt-water licenses from the state are required and can be purchased for a certain number of days or annually. Pompano is a local delicacy, and you may also catch redfish and bluefish. To prevent accidents please do not fish close to where people are swimming.

■ The Beach Experience

Stark white sand dunes give way to the shoreline, the transition zone leading to the sparkling waters that mix and mingle colors of blue, aqua,
turquoise, and green. The effect is slightly mesmerizing, but take care that
the abundant natural beauty does not lull you into a false sense of security.
Like a lovely rose this enticing creation of nature has a few thorns that you
must consider.

Winter wave action pulls sand off the beach and creates underwater sand-
bars that can give a false impression of depth. After taking a few steps, you
may find yourself in very deep water. Then in summer the sand is returned
to the beach in an endless cycle. When swimming on the ocean side of the
island, be aware of rip tides and currents, especially where children are concerned. The currents can gradually sweep even the strongest of adult swimmers into trouble on occasion. Caution should also be exercised as the water
may contain jellyfish, sea nettles, and Portuguese man-of-wars. All have
stinging tentacles and are not poisonous, but can definitely ruin your day. If
you suddenly find yourself in a school of small fish, they are probably being
pursued by a predator, which may be a much larger fish, and you will be wise
to leave the water for a while. In summer months sunburn is a very real con-
cern, and you should apply a strong sunscreen every time you come out of
the water. Drink plenty of fresh water to replace what you will loose while
exercising in the heat and stay out of the water during thunderstorms:
Florida has the highest occurrence of lightning in the United States.

Even with all these precautions, it is possible to experience a lovely day
on the beaches of the Gulf Island National Seashore. Enjoy an evening
swim in the ocean during the months of July and August, and you may be
fortunate enough to see glowing plankton floating in the water. Notice the
area where sand meets water, it is rich with life. Tiny sand crabs scurry
about in search of food. As each wave recedes from the shore, a slurry of
sand, pebbles, and shells shifts with the motion, revealing tiny sand-
dwelling crustaceans that feed on microscopic prey. Seabirds pluck these
creatures from the sand in the natural progression of the food chain.

If shell collecting is your passion, be advised that these beaches are not
renowned for shelling, as is Sanibel Island, for instance, but careful scrutiny can bring some interesting results. Small shells that are common to the

Santa Rosa Island.

area are the lettered olive, common Atlantic marginella, salt marsh snail, and coquinas. The tulip mussel is not as common on this coast as on others, but it may be found around rock jetties built at harbor entrances for surf control. Atlantic cockle, Tampa drills, and sharp-ribbed drills may be found onshore after a winter storm, which is the best time for shelling. Low tide will be your most successful time; do not overlook any tidepools you may find. Take only those shells that are empty—the occupied shells are protected by the NPS. Return them to the water. (In the "Additional Reading" section of this book are listings for two shelling field guides that can help in identifying your shells. The field guide by Jean Andrews offers some excellent tips on cleaning and preserving empty shells, which should be done as soon as possible.)

Offshore you may see a flock of brown pelicans feeding on a school of fish, or the fins of dolphins gliding gracefully through the water. Among the more playful creatures in the sea, dolphins often swim ahead of fishing boats in the Gulf, as if leading them to their destinations. They usually keep their distance but may come close when you are swimming in the Gulf. Do not fear them for dolphins are the best friends you can have in this water.

Many people enjoy simply observing the ocean and its awesome power.

Perhaps in the relentless conflict of the beach, between wind, wave, and sand, we can forget our own problems for a brief period. Sit for a while to ruminate on the meaning of life as the sun sets to the west, spreading warm pink and orange rays across the surface of the white sand, mixing and mingling with deep purple shadows from the dunes. The impression is one of tranquility. These ancient shores call to you to pause and contemplate, dig your toes into the sand, and enjoy a small modicum of peace that is all too difficult to find in our everyday lives. Finish your day with an evening cookout in one of the

Glades morning glory, Santa Rosa Island.

pavilions as the sun drops below the horizon, and this will surely be one of the most memorable events of your national seashore experience.

■ Information

ACCESS: There are several points of access for Santa Rosa Island: From downtown Fort Walton Beach, follow Highway 98 eastward across Brooks Bridge and continue across the island. Or proceed westward on Highway 98 to the Navarre area, where Highway 87 intersects Highway 98, turning left (south) over the toll bridge, then right (west) on State Road 399 along the island.

From Pensacola take Highway 98 east through the Gulf Breeze community, then south on State Road 399. Cross the toll bridge to the first intersection, then right on Fort Pickens Road or follow State Road 399 to the left for the Opal Beach unit.

BEST TIME TO VISIT: The high tourist season is the summer months from

Memorial Day through Labor Day, but for any activity other than swimming and sunbathing, spring and fall are the best times to visit. Even the winter months are not very cold here and can be very enjoyable. Gone are the hordes of tourists, the stifling heat and humidity, and most of the insects.

Yellow-eyed grass in bloom, Santa Rosa Island.

CAMPING AND LODGING: Camping is a bit difficult to locate and usually more remote here. Near Fort Pickens on the western end of the island is a 200-site campground with camp store and laundry facilities. Reservations are accepted, and it fills quickly, especially during the summer season. Contact the NPS reservation system at (800) 365–CAMP. Visitor centers at Naval Live Oaks and Fort Pickens can advise about alternate campgrounds in the area. Camping facilities include the following:

- Crystal Beach RV Park, 2825 Highway 98 East, Destin; (850) 837–6447

- Holiday Travel Park, 5380 Highway 98 East, Destin; (850) 837–6334

- Playground RV Park, 777 Beal Parkway, Fort Walton Beach; (850) 862–3513

- Emerald Beach Campground, Highway 98 (1 mile east of Highway 87 junction), Navarre: 77 sites; (850) 939–3431

- Magnolia Beach Campground, Highway 98 (3.5 miles east of Highway 87 junction), Navarre; 60 sites; (850) 939–2717

- Navarre Beach Campground, 9201 Navarre Parkway, Navarre; 150 sites; (850) 939–2188

Numerous hotels and motels can be located in the commercially devel-

Human negligence, a major problem, Pensacola.

oped areas and will be within reasonable driving distances from the GINS facilities. Among the lodgings are the following:

- Days Inn, 573 Santa Rosa Boulevard, Fort Walton Beach; (850) 244–8686

- Park Inn, Miracle Strip Parkway, Fort Walton Beach; (850) 244–0121

- Radisson Beach Resort, 1110 Santa Rosa Boulevard, Fort Walton Beach; (850) 243–9181

- Best Western Hotel, Highway 98 East, Navarre; (850) 939–9400

- Comfort Inn, 8700 Navarre Parkway, Navarre; (850) 939–1761

OTHER INFORMATION: All facilities at the Opal Beach area are wheelchair accessible. The day-use facility at Opal Beach has an entry fee that is good for seven days and is accepted at any of the other fee areas. An annual pass is available at a slightly higher fee and allows unlimited access during daylight hours. Covered picnic shelters feature charcoal grills, but open fires are prohibited. Pets are allowed in designated campgrounds and nature trails,

Sunning and fishing, Navarre.

but only while on a leash and under physical control. They are prohibited in all beach areas and picnic areas. No boat launching facilities are provided here, but are available 4 miles to the east at Navarre.

Each September the park hosts a "Beach Clean-Up Day." Volunteers are welcome and encouraged. If you would like to get involved and do your part to maintain these glorious shores as nature intended, please contact the National Park Service office at the Naval Live Oaks unit; (850) 934–2600.

In case of emergency call 911 or the NPS dispatch office at (850) 651–7400.

You'll find a Gulf Islands Web site with more information to help plan your park visit at www.nps.gov/guis/.

If you are not the spontaneous type and tend to plan every detail in advance, you will like the following Web site, which is remarkably comprehensive and features hundreds of links to other helpful sites: www.access-gulfcoast.com.

NEARBY POINTS OF INTEREST, OKALOOSA AREA

Just east of the island's tip, across the bridge, is Destin, Florida, which proclaims itself "Fishing Capital of the World." The city's docks are home to an enormous sport-fishing fleet, and there are charters to suit anyone's needs. Each October the city hosts a giant fishing rodeo with numerous prizes for several categories of game fish. For information call (850) 837–1981 or visit these Web sites: www.destinfl.com/fishing; www.fishing destinflorida.com.

The Gulfarium, in Fort Walton Beach features a variety of sea life in several daily shows; (850) 243–9046.

You are never far away from a golf course on the Gulf Coast.

■ Golf Club of Destin, 12958 Highway 98 West, Destin; (850) 837–7422

■ Indian Bayou Country Club, 1 Country Club Drive East, Destin; (850) 837–6191

■ Fort Walton Beach Golf Club, 1909 Lewis Turner Boulevard, Fort Walton Beach; (850) 833–9528

NEARBY POINTS OF INTEREST, OPAL BEACH AREA

At the Navarre Visitor Center on Highway 98 is The Panhandle Butterfly House, which is worth a visit. These beautiful creatures float about and will actually land on your shoulder as you walk through the enclosed structure. The Butterfly House is closed in winter months.

The state of Florida has an excellent state park system with several units in close proximity to Santa Rosa Island. An informative brochure, *Florida State Parks: The Real Florida* can be obtained by calling (850) 488–9872, or check the Web site at www.dep.state.fl.us/parks.

PHOTO TIPS: Special precautions are in order in any beach environment, and this one is no exception. You will not see the fine particles of sand floating on the wind, but be advised that they exist and are deadly to the inner workings of your electronic camera and accessories. If possible, walk back to your vehicle and change the film inside its protective cabin. If you must open the camera back or change lenses on the beach, do so under a towel or inside a beach bag. Clean your lens frequently with a soft brush. Do not wipe with a cloth as you might scratch the glass.

All that beautiful white sand will fool your camera meter into underexposing your images, and it will be necessary to set the compensation device for one to one and one-half stops *more* exposure (overexposure) when you see a viewfinder full of white. Use your flash unit when photographing human faces to eliminate dark shadows in their eye sockets or under the bill of a hat. Most new cameras will compensate automatically and correct for the red-eye syndrome.

Fort Pickens

The Fort Pickens area is located at the western end of Santa Rosa Island; it is the most visited of the Gulf Islands National Seashore facilities on Santa Rosa Island.

The approach via Fort Pickens Road is along a narrow spit of land that has been ravaged by hurricanes in recent years, and an intensive campaign has been instituted to restore the dunes. No stopping or parking is allowed until you reach the information center/ranger station on the main body of the island. The facility includes beach access, fishing pier, nature and walking trails, and a Civil War–era fort to be explored.

This end of the island has a long and varied past stemming back to before the time of early Spanish exploration. A tiny Spanish outpost, probably the first European settlement on the island, was established circa 1723 and was demolished by a hurricane in 1754. Archeological studies have shown that even before that, the island was home to many Native American villages. Shell middens that were unearthed indicate that these aboriginals survived on a diet of shellfish, such as mollusks, oysters, and clams.

Your exploration should begin just inside the main gate. The first point of interest is the structure housing the Ranger Station. This building dates back to the beginning of the twentieth century when it was a Coast Guard rescue station. From here long "surf boats" were launched and rowed by powerful oarsmen to aid ships in distress in the Pensacola Bay area. The ranger office displays vintage photographs depicting such rescue activities and the building's original appearance. This structure has experienced numerous facelifts, most recently in 1995 when two hurricanes in the same

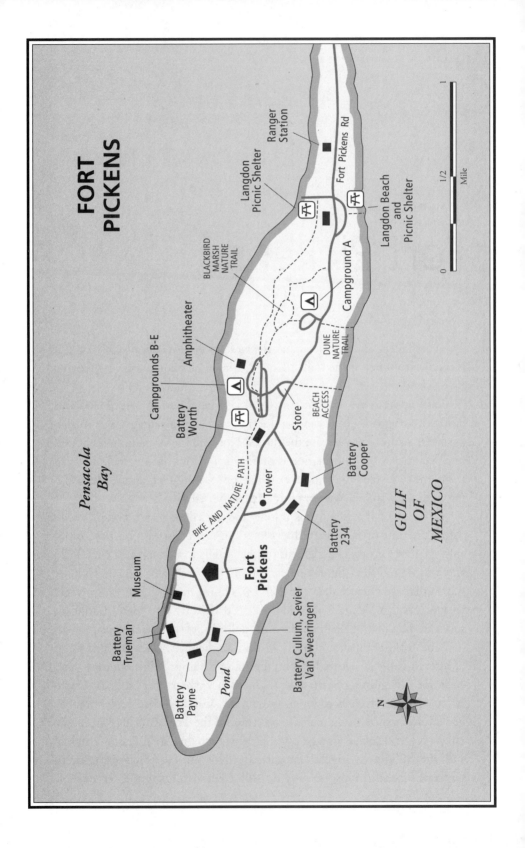

FORT PICKENS

Pensacola Bay

Battery Trueman

Battery Payne

Pond

Museum

Battery Cullum, Sevier Van Swearingen

Fort Pickens

Battery 234

Battery Cooper

• Tower

BIKE AND NATURE PATH

Campgrounds B-E

Battery Worth

Amphitheater

Store

BEACH ACCESS

DUNE NATURE TRAIL

BLACKBIRD MARSH NATURE TRAIL

Campground A

Langdon Picnic Shelter

Fort Pickens Rd

Ranger Station

Langdon Beach and Picnic Shelter

GULF OF MEXICO

N

0   1/2   1   Mile

Fort Pickens, Pensacola.

season caused extensive damage, closing this unit for nine months. The buildings were quickly repaired, but the dune restoration has continued into the new millennium.

A short drive along the main road leads to Battery Langdon on the right. Originally completed in 1923, it mounted two 12-inch guns and is among nine concrete batteries completed on Santa Rosa Island. War Department hysteria over the Japanese bombing of Pearl Harbor prompted this earthen camouflaged bunker to be further fortified with a concrete roof seventeen feet thick during World War II! Live oaks have since grown all around the facility and do an adequate job of camouflage in their own right. The weaponry has long since been removed, but a roadside exhibit describes the original gun emplacements.

To the right of Battery Langdon is the beginning of an unpaved road that leads to the Langdon picnic area, located near the bay side of the island. Directly across the road, Langdon Beach offers access to the shore via a boardwalk over the dunes, a covered pavilion with bathrooms, and exterior showers for swimmers.

Farther along is the Dune Nature Trail, a boardwalk with exhibits that crosses natural habitat and continues on to the beach. Across the main road is the entrance to the group camping area, available by reservation for large groups of any type. A lovely campground for individuals has been established at Fort Pickens and is situated in an inviting pine forest that offers shade from the incessant daytime sun. The entrance to Loop A is the next road to the right, past the group camping area.

A 2.2-mile bike and walking trail begins at Battery Langdon and traverses the campgrounds, then passes the picnic grounds and gun emplacements at Battery Worth, and crosses an interesting wetland area before continuing on to the fort at the tip of the island. Remember that this is a barrier island, and the marsh areas on both sides of the trail are typical, interior, brackish-water wetlands that support a variety of wildlife. So if you see any wild animals, please keep your distance and do not attempt to feed them. This unnamed trail is the eastern terminus of the Florida National Scenic Trail (see "Other Information" at the end of this chapter) and follows the bed of an old narrow-gauge railroad that was used to transport personnel

and supplies to the various military sites on the island. Be advised that bikes may be ridden on the main road and all side roads, in addition to this trail, but they are not allowed on the beaches or the boardwalk approaches.

The Blackbird Marsh Nature Trail begins at the rear of campground Loop A (foot traffic only) and offers an interesting, if very brief, walk through typical island marsh habitat. Farther along Fort Pickens Road is the camp store and entrance to the main body of the campground, Loops B through E.

Unlike the Opal Beach area, this western end of the island shows much evidence of the hand of humans. European explorers began a

Antique cannon, Fort Pickens, Pensacola.

lengthy struggle for control of this area as early as 1559 when Spain established a settlement at Pensacola Bay, which was abandoned soon afterward. Spaniards revived the settlement in 1698, surrendered it to the French in 1719, then regained it by treaty in 1722. It was then ceded to England in 1763 and retaken by force in 1781. When Florida finally became part of the United States, in 1825, the government began to develop Pensacola as a major naval base with fortifications, including Fort Pickens.

Named for Brigadier General Andrew Pickens of South Carolina, who served in the War for Independence, the fort saw some action as a federal fortification during the Civil War. In 1861 its artillery bombarded the Confederate-held Fort Barrancas (also part of the national seashore) just across the bay on the mainland, and Fort McRee on Perdido Key. Fort McRee was practically obliterated and subsequent erosion has removed all trace of its presence, but Barrancas, on the grounds of the Pensacola Naval Station, has been restored and maintained.

The original construction at Fort Pickens is a marvel of craftsmanship. Millions of handmade bricks were laid in huge arched configurations several feet thick to support the big-gun emplacements on top, while allowing easy passageway for soldiers underneath. The fort was constructed in a pentagonal shape with bastions located at all five corners, each with its own guns and served by three magazines. The bastions protruded outward from the wall line allowing gunners to set up a crossfire with the opposing bastions to repel attackers. When visiting the fort, you will want to spend some time exploring the intricate tunnels that extend underground to rifle ports and munitions storage rooms. As you explore remember that all building materials and workers had to be transported to the site by barge, across the mouth of the bay, and imagine the hardships involved.

The concrete battery that looks so incongruous compared with the rest of the fort is Battery Pensacola. It was added in 1899. It mounted two 12-inch guns on disappearing carriages that could deliver 1,070-pound shells over a range of 8 miles. Guided tours of the fort are conducted daily, and candlelight tours are scheduled spring through fall. Schedules are posted at all GINS visitor centers.

Over the succeeding years Fort Pickens was expanded and updated with modern cannon that present a stark contrast to the older guns that have

Sand live oaks, Fort Pickens Area, Pensacola.

been restored to the original building. Further gun emplacements were constructed in the form of satellite batteries scattered about the island, camouflaged in earthen mounds. Battery 234 (built in 1943), Battery Worth (built in 1899), Battery Payne (built in 1904), Battery Van Swearingen (built in 1898), and Battery Langdon have long been disabled but left intact, and the huge cannon in some are of interest to awestruck kids of all ages. Battery Cooper (built in 1905), which had two different types of gun emplacements during its tenure, is open for exploration of its exhibits at varying times. Adjacent to Fort Pickens is what appears to be a single large emplacement, but it is actually two individual batteries, Cullum and Sevier, which had separate firing controls and were completed in 1898. Battery Trueman was built in 1905 at the mouth of the harbor entrance, and mounted two 3-inch rapid-fire guns to defend the channel from minesweepers and torpedo boats. All these defenses were declared surplus in 1947 and were deactivated.

West of the entrance to the Battery Worth picnic area, across from the entrance to Batteries 234 and Cooper, is a small fenced area that is the fam-

Armament and bunker, Battery 234, Fort Pickens Area, Pensacola.

ily cemetery of Major William H. Chase. Major Chase supervised the construction of the four forts in the area. It was moved here from Chasefield Plantation, on the mainland, when the Pensacola Naval Yard took over the property that was his home.

An extremely interesting museum exists in an auditorium located among the personnel housing in the center of the fort compound. Interactive exhibits at the museum are intended to educate as well as inform and cover the great variety of wildlife and plant life indigenous to the area. A separate room is dedicated to Civil War and World War II activities and the imprisonment at Fort Pickens of the famous Apache Indian chief, Geronimo.

Fort Pickens was deactivated following the Civil War. Technological advances in weaponry during the last half of the nineteenth century made the forts at Pensacola obsolete, and they sat idle, deteriorating in the elements. But residents of Pensacola, desperate to pump new life into their city, seized an opportunity when Geronimo was captured on the western frontier. In a petition to President Grover Cleveland, they successfully argued that Fort Pickens was an alternative to execution, and the Indian prisoners quickly became a tourist attraction.

The once proud leader of the Chiricahua Apaches and his small band were exposed to public inspection and humiliation for some eighteen months. Hundreds of visitors crossed the bay by boat and trudged across the sand to see these curious prisoners who had eluded capture for so long. Even after the Apaches were transferred to another location, the curious still came for many years. They would stare in wonder as guides at the fort pointed out a dank and dark cell that was supposed to have held the prisoners; it was, in fact, a lie. Geronimo's captors knew that he could not swim, and with no other means of escape from the island, he and his followers were allowed to roam the grounds at will.

The museum is open daily and is free of additional charge. Park personnel present periodic programs at the museum. Check at the office or bulletin boards for dates and details.

Fort Pickens has a very popular fishing pier on the bay side that fills up early on suitable days, and appropriate saltwater fishing licenses from the state are required to fish there. Near-shore fishing with live bait is most productive in April and May. Redfish, pompano, speckled trout, and bluefish are abundant in these waters, and local bait shops can tell you what is being caught at the time of your visit and also recommend tackle that you will need.

■ The Trails at Fort Pickens

The abundant evidence of human intrusion notwithstanding, this small park still offers amazing opportunities for the solitary enjoyment of nature. Blackbird Marsh Nature Trail and the Dune Nature Trail are short, but the longer trail running from the campground to the fort offers more possibilities. This trail is open to bicycles and passes through the lovely Battery Worth picnic area, which has individual and group facilities.

A historical marker in the Battery Worth area commemorates the William Bartram Trail. This noted explorer and naturalist explored the area extensively from 1773 to 1776 and wrote lyrical prose about the land, the people, and the ecosystem in his journal: "It [Pensacola] is delightfully situated upon gentle rising ascents environing a spacious harbour, safe and capacious enough to shelter all the navies of Europe, and excellent ground for anchorage; the West End of St. Rose [Santa Rosa] Island stretches across the great bay St. Maria Galves, [Pensacola Bay] and its south-west projecting point forms the harbor of Pensacola, which, with the road or entrance, is defended by a block-house built on the extremity of that point, which at the same time serves the purpose of a fortress and look-out tower."

Bartram's highly detailed journals were later published in book form. Much of the plant life that Bartram wrote so effusively about in his journals is still present for viewing today. Take a quiet walk along one of the trails and observe native plant life including spartina, saw palmetto, and Florida rosemary (no relation to the herb) any time of year. Fall and winter bring the yellow blooms of camphorweed to brighten your day and attract the monarch butterflies, which migrate through the area in October. In spring and summer wild flowers such as sedge, duck potato, and glades morning glory bloom in profusion along with other species capable of surviving the high salt content of the environment, growing in precious pockets of soil when sufficient moisture is present. But beware of the coast sandspur during all seasons. Its tiny balls of sharp-pointed spurs can inflict much pain to bare feet while walking the beach.

Many of the dunes are covered in what appears, at first glance, to be a hedge of some sort. It grows low and spreads widely, often covering most of the smaller dunes. This is in fact the live oak tree struggling to survive under disadvantageous conditions and is now considered a separate species, the sand live oak (*Quercus geminata*). These dwarfed trees occupy the secondary dunes behind those nearest the ocean, and when they attain a height that exceeds that of the primary dunes, wind-borne salt spray dries out the upper reaches of the limbs, eventually killing them. Because the tree cannot grow upward, it spreads outward instead, offering another instance of Nature's uncanny ability to adapt. Notice how some of these trees have a pronounced lean toward the mainland, a result of "salt shearing" during their growth by the relentless onshore winds.

Nature lovers will notice many more unusual plants on this island, such as the marsh mallow that grows in the wetland areas. You guessed it: The roots of this plant were once cooked to produce the original snack food we love to roast over an open fire in the campground.

The avian enthusiast has not been forgotten on Santa Rosa Island. As you walk the trails notice that the overhead canopy is alive with birdsong.

Dune restoration area, Pensacola.

Visitors may include mockingbirds, swallows, red-winged blackbirds, cardinals, and blue jays. Look carefully and you just might see the elusive rufous-sided towhee.

Spring and fall are favorite bird-watching times for the significant migrations that pass through the islands. When the weather turns cold in northern climes, birds migrate southward to these shores (as do the human residents of northern climes. The similarity of these actions has not escaped this author!). The barrier islands are the last resting and feeding areas for tanagers, warblers, and grosbeaks before leaving on their autumn crossing southward over the Gulf of Mexico, and they must store fat for the journey. Usually they depart at sundown when offshore winds aid their flight.

In spring the islands are the first landfall for exhausted migrators that have flown, nonstop, for 600 miles or more over open water. At a flying speed of approximately thirty miles per hour, the songbirds are in the air for fifteen hours with no rest, food, or water. They maintain an elevation of approximately 3,000 feet or more and are subject to predation along the way from hawks, eagles, and other raptors that share the airspace. The most fascinating of the transgulf migrators are the diminutive ruby-throated hummingbirds, which weigh barely an ounce or two and normally need to feed on a continuing basis due to the high metabolic rate of their systems. How any of them survive the crossing is one of nature's many intriguing secrets.

Park personnel organize bird-watching and wildflower walks during migration seasons, in which visitors are invited to participate. Schedules are subject to change, so check with the visitor centers.

Bird and wildflower guidebooks will add immensely to the enjoyment of your walk on the trails even if you are not an avid naturalist.

■ You Can Help

Scientists band migrating birds in an attempt to unravel the secrets of this mysterious behavior; what drives them to make these long journeys, often at the expense of their lives? How do they navigate at night and in bad weather? Observers like you can help to answer these questions and more. When a banded bird is close enough, note the exact color sequence on each leg. If injured, record the numbers on the band, and if dead remove the bands and return to the U.S. Fish and Wildlife Service. There is no need to identify the species, but include the date and location you found the bird, its condition (alive, injured, released), and finally, your name and mailing address.

Send any information you have to the following address:

Bird Banding Laboratory
U.S. Fish and Wildlife Service
Washington, DC　(no zip code is required)

They will write you with any information they have on the bird that you found. If you enjoy bird-watching, you will probably enjoy doing your part to assist this research.

Stunted growth pine tree on beach, Fort Pickens.

■ Information

ACCESS: From Pensacola take Highway 98 east through the Gulf Breeze community, then south on SR 399, then right on Fort Pickens Road.

BEST TIME TO VISIT: To a great extent when it's best to visit depends on what activities interest you. Anytime but summer is quite pleasant on the island, and camping space will be readily available. But if you want to swim and work on your tan, then the summer season is for you, but expect congestion, heat and humidity, and insects.

CAMPING AND LODGING: A public campground is located on site with all amenities, including a camp store located at the entrance. This 200-space facility fills up quickly in summer, and reservations are accepted up to five months in advance by calling (800) 365–2267. Campground registration is at the ranger station, the first structure you encounter after the entrance station. Alternate campgrounds are located back on the mainland, along Highway 98. The ranger station has directions to them.

Several major motels are located at Pensacola Beach and Gulf Breeze including:

- Holiday Inn, 51 Gulf Breeze Parkway, Gulf Breeze; (850) 932–2214

- Best Western Inn, 16 Via de Luna Drive, Pensacola Beach; (850) 934–3300

- Clarion Suites, 20 Via de Luna Drive, Pensacola Beach; (850) 932–4300

- Hampton Inn, 2 Via de Luna Drive, Pensacola Beach; (850) 932–6800

OTHER INFORMATION: An admission fee is charged and is good for seven days of unlimited entrances and exits to all park units. For a slightly higher fee, an annual permit is available, offering unlimited access to the facilities for one year.

The posted speed limit is stringently enforced, so please drive carefully as there will likely be people strolling or riding bikes along the main road. A stop at the information center/ranger station is recommended for maps of the area and directions. Attendants can also assist with camping or lodging accommodations, fishing information, other nearby attractions, and a cold drink of water.

A museum, gift shop, public rest rooms, and a small snack shop are located on the grounds of the fort. Various interpretive programs are scheduled throughout the year and a seasonal activity schedule is published and made available at all visitor centers.

The campground store is open seasonally and offers the basic staples, but nothing of a gourmet nature. Better shopping is available back in the Pensacola Beach area. A bank of public telephones is located outside the camp store.

A Web site is available at www.nps.gov/guis/ with more information to help you plan your visit.

Information—and a map—on the remainder of the Florida National Scenic Trail can be obtained from the Florida Trail Association, P.O. Box 13708, Gainesville, FL, 32604; (800) 343–1882.

NEARBY POINTS OF INTEREST: The Opal Beach unit is approximately 10 to 12 miles east along Highway 399. The Naval Live Oaks unit is across the sound on the mainland on U.S. Highway 98. The Fort

Cannons and interior, Fort Pickens.

Barrancas and Advance Redoubt units are across the bay at the Pensacola Naval Air Station.

Golf courses are prevalent in the Pensacola area. Here are a few:

- Tiger Point Country Club, 1255 Country Club, Gulf Breeze; (850) 932–1333, (800) 477–4833

- The Club at Hidden Creek, 3070 PGA Boulevard, Navarre; (850) 939–4604

- Creekside Golf Club, 5555 Esperanto Drive, Pensacola; (850) 944–7969

- Marcus Pointe Golf Club, 2500 Oak Pointe Drive, Pensacola; (850) 484–9770, (800) 3–MARCUS

- Osceola Golf Club, 300 Tonawanda Drive, Pensacola; (850) 453–7599

- Scenic Hills Country Club, 8891 Burning Tree Road, Pensacola; (850) 476–0611, (800) 477–4833

■ Lost Key Golf Club, 625 Lost Key Drive, Perdido Key; (850)
492–1300, (888) 2–LOSTKEY

The state of Florida has an excellent state park system with several units
in close proximity to Santa Rosa Island. An informative brochure, *Florida
State Parks: The Real Florida* can be obtained by calling (850) 488–9872, or
check the Web site at www.dep.state.fl.us/parks.

PHOTO TIPS: The brick arches of the fort can be used to advantage in your
photographic compositions. A wide-angle lens will exaggerate the perspec-
tive to create pictures of interest to your family and friends back home. Light
levels will be very low inside the various buildings, and even when using
high-speed film, a tripod will be very useful in achieving sharp images.

On the beach take extraordinary measures to protect your camera from
airborne sand particles. Exposure compensation (overexposure) will probably be required when you see abundant white sand in your viewfinder to
prevent drastically underexposed pictures. When photographing people,
use your flash unit, even on a bright, sunny beach day. It will fill in the light
in those eye sockets and shadows from hats.

Fort Barrancas

Pensacola's name was derived from the Panzacola Indians, now extinct, who lived in the area when the first Spanish explorers arrived. Considered a strategic location since the first white men set foot on land there, many nations, including Spain, France, and Great Britain, would struggle for control of the bay area over the years. While suffering with yellow fever and enduring vicious storms, they would build crude fortifications in what is now the Barrancas area and later abandon them.

In many ways the history of Barrancas parallels the history of Pensacola Bay. Due to the vagaries of records kept by early Spanish explorers, it is not known who actually discovered the bay area. As early as 1519 Alonso Alvárez de Pineda coasted the entire Gulf of Florida and may have visited the bay. In 1528 it is possible that remnants of the ill-fated Narváez expedition may have taken shelter in the bay coastal area, but records indicate that de Soto's men definitely visited in 1539.

The best-organized expedition was led by Tristán de Luna y Arellano. He arrived in Pensacola Bay on August 14, 1559 with thirteen ships bearing 1,000 colonists and 500 soldiers to establish a colony, only to be met by almost immediate disaster. On August 19 a vicious hurricane from the Gulf entered the bay area and sunk most of his ships, killing the majority of the people and destroying all the supplies meant to last for a year. One of the surviving ships was sent back to home port for help, and the surviving soldiers scattered inland in search of food. After a year's time, when rescue finally came, two-thirds of the original expedition had disappeared, and

67

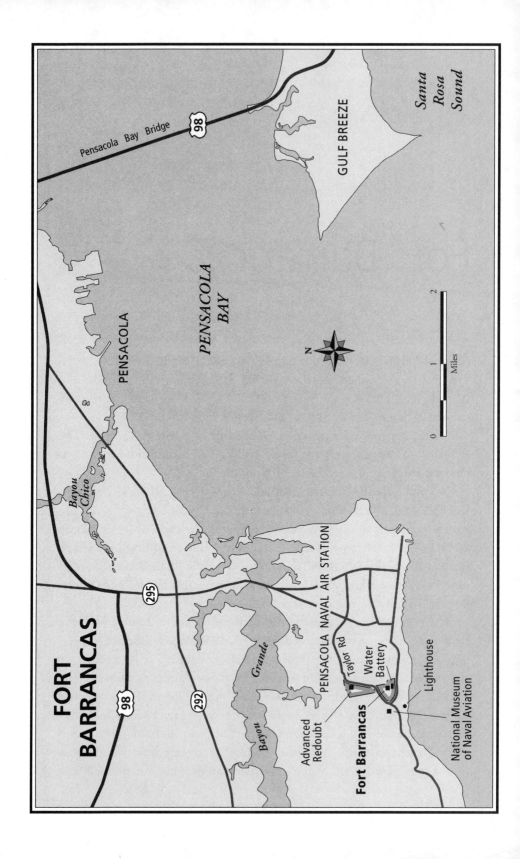

Fort Barrancas, Pensacola.

Luna had fallen ill. The site, believed to have been in the area of the location of the present-day Fort Barrancas, was finally abandoned in 1561.

Although it is now located on forty-eight acres of the Pensacola Naval Air Station, the present structure, Fort Barrancas, is in fact a unit of the Gulf Islands National Seashore. Another fort that figured prominently in the Civil War, it is located on a high promontory overlooking the mouth of Pensacola Bay and Fort Pickens across the way. So pleasant and serene is the setting that it is practically impossible to imagine Federal and Confederate forces shelling each other from these two forts during the regrettable Civil War.

The unique name is derived from the Spanish word, *barranca*, meaning "bluff." English explorers built a fort on this location in 1763. It was captured by the Spanish in 1781 and named San Carlos de Barrancas. When Florida became a U.S. possession, the decision was made to build forts on all the land points at the mouth of the bay in order to protect the Naval Yard. In addition to Barrancas and Pickens, there would be McRee at the tip of Fosters Island, now known as Perdido Key, and the Advanced Redoubt inland to ward off any land based attack on Barrancas. The structure in front of the fort, called the Water Battery, was the original Spanish fortification, and the arrangement of the U.S. fort would incorporate it into the final design of Fort Barrancas.

Beginning in 1829 the construction project would continue for thirty years. When complete, the fortifications were considered impregnable, so there was no reason for them to be manned except by skeleton crews. That was the official explanation at least; in truth, the United States never had enough troops to garrison the forts. Here is another interesting fact: In this period just prior to the Civil War, the United States authorized construction of the forts by a contractor that used slave labor. Ironically the only action the forts would ever see would be in the Civil War when Americans fought each other. None of the forts would ever receive their full complement of weaponry, and during the Civil War, ironclad ships and the more powerful cannon that were developed eventually made masonry forts obsolete.

Barrancas was completed in 1844, and when a battalion was sent to occupy it in 1848, they were shocked by what they found. The battalion commander complained that there were no facilities for cooking and washing or caring for the sick. So strong were troop complaints that, in 1850, appropriations were finally made for the construction of barracks.

The present structure at Barrancas has seen a more thorough restoration than has Fort Pickens, but only one cannon of the era graces a rampart that was intended to mount nineteen. As with Fort Pickens, the architectural detail of Fort Barrancas is a marvel to behold. Incredible numbers of handmade brick were crafted into what must surely have been the most impregnable fortress of its time. The design is in the shape of a modified triangle and includes a dry moat encircling two sides of the structure—dry because the sandy soil will not hold water. A retractable wooden drawbridge across the moat allowed access to the only entrance. The main building has a continuous line of rifle ports facing the moat, and a similar structure rings the outside of the moat. Any enemy that ventured into the moat would have been trapped in a deadly crossfire by rifle and cannon before having any chance of scaling the walls of the main building. Reminiscent of a catacomb, a tunnel from the fort leading under the moat allowed soldiers safe access to the outer rifle gallery. Barrancas is a labyrinth of tunnels highlighted by the warm Florida sun peeking through its rifle ports. Not only Civil War buffs, but anyone with an avocation for history will find it a most interesting exploration. This fort has fewer visitors than Fort Pickens, perhaps due to the difficulty of locating it, but it is well worth the trip to see the completely restored structure and the lovely moss-draped live oak trees on the grounds at the naval base.

■ Touring the Fort

A visitor center and gift shop, where free guides to the fort are available, are located at the entrance to the grounds. Just outside is a display of cannon that demonstrates some of the various types of weaponry employed during hostilities in the area. The short-barreled cannon were developed in France and England and brought here by the early settlers. Their purpose was to lob cannonballs up and over the armored sides of ships and forts and onto the decks or fort's interiors, which were more easily damaged.

Walking up the path to the fort, you are confronted with an impressive earthen embankment that hid the fort from land-based attacks. Before entering the structure, notice the counterscarp gallery, the outer structure of the dry moat, with its rifle ports facing the main building. The drawbridge, which was raised by winch and counterweight, allows visitors access to the "sally port," the main entrance, which was guarded by heavy oak doors. Inside and to the right is the guardroom where soldiers assembled; straight ahead is the parade ground, the center of the fort, that once held a furnace for heating of cannonballs. The view seaward from the parade ground is quite impressive. Varying shades of green water contrast sharply with the snow-white sand, and Fort Pickens is visible just across the bay. On the opposite side of the parade ground is a tunnel that allows safe passage to the Spanish-built

Escarpment interior, Fort Barrancas, Pensacola.

Cannon display at Fort Barrancas, Pensacola.

Water Battery outside, so named because its guns could ricochet shot off the water to strike ships near water level. The whitewashed structure features some authentic Spanish architectural embellishments that were restored based on drawings and fragments.

Just off the main gate are entrances to the scarp gallery, which rings the structure with rifle ports facing out toward the moat. Six million brick were employed in the construction of these walls, which are four feet thick. Roam about the gallery tunnels as you please and wonder at the confined space in which the soldiers were expected to operate. Imagine trying to load a long-barreled musket with a packing rod in such a space. You cannot get lost, the sally port is the only exit, and all tunnels return to that location. The fort became a part of the national seashore in 1971, and following a 1.2 million-dollar restoration, it was reopened to the public by the National Park Service in 1980. Guided tours are regularly scheduled, and several special programs dealing with the fort's history are presented at various times during the summer months. Schedules are posted at the visitor centers.

While in the area, be sure to visit the Pensacola Lighthouse, which was built in the same era. When the U.S. Navy decided in 1824 to construct its first deepwater port on the Gulf Coast at Pensacola, a light was needed to guide ships in and out of the harbor.

The first tower constructed was only eighty feet above sea level and proved to be insufficient. The current 210-foot tower was built of brick in 1858. The light-keepers quarters are below. Henri LaPaite created its Fresnel lens in Paris. It is six feet in diameter, hand-cut and polished, and capable of casting a beam up to 20 miles out to sea. The lens is still in use today, although the light has been automated and no attendant is required. The base of the tower has brick walls six feet thick, which show evidence of cracks made during the Civil War when cannon shot hammered the tower. The hurricane of 1874 also damaged the tower, but it was subsequently repaired and is as structurally sound today as ever. Guided tours are available on weekends during the summer months. Check with NPS personnel at the Barrancas Visitor Center for times and details.

■ Information

ACCESS: From Pensacola take Highway 292 west, turn left (south) on Highway 295, cross Bayou Grande, and enter the Pensacola Naval Air Station main gate via the far right-hand lane. The guard should wave you on through, but if stopped, simply advise that you are visiting the national seashore facilities and then follow the signs.

BEST TIME TO VISIT: Anytime of year is fine for visiting, except during time of national emergency, when admittance may possibly be denied. Because you will not be participating in water sports, spring, winter, or fall are recommended, as the weather will be more comfortable. This facility is open seven days a week, except at Christmas; hours vary seasonally.

CAMPING AND LODGING: In the Pensacola area, camping is available at the following locations:

■ Mayfair RV Park, 4540 Mobile Highway; (850) 455–8561

■ Timberlake RV Park, 2600 West Michigan Avenue; (850) 944–5487

Farther west on Highway 292 is the Big Lagoon State Park with camping available. Call (850) 492–1595 for information and reservations.

Lodging is abundant in the Pensacola area with all major hotel and motel chains represented. When making reservations, request the locations closest to the naval air station.

■ Days Inn, 7051 Pensacola Boulevard, Pensacola; (850) 476–9090, (800) 325–2525

■ Hampton Inn, 2187 Airport Boulevard, Pensacola; (850) 478–1123, (800) HAMPTON

■ Holiday Inn Express, 6501 Pensacola Boulevard, Pensacola; (850) 476–7200, (800) HOLIDAY

■ Motel 6, 5829 Pensacola Boulevard, Pensacola; (850) 477–7522, (800) 466–8356

The central business district offers an excellent assortment of restaurants, shops, and entertainment.

OTHER INFORMATION: You'll find a well-shaded picnic ground located behind the visitor center and a short nature trail across the parking lot. The trail offers a pleasant walk through heavily shaded terrain, but there is no printed guide or exhibits.

There is no entrance fee at Fort Barrancas or the Pensacola Naval Air Station gate. While driving on naval station property, you are under jurisdiction of the U.S. Navy and subject to federal prosecution for infractions, so please drive wisely and carefully.

A Web site is available at www.nps.gov/guis/ with more information to help plan your visit.

NEARBY POINTS OF INTEREST: The Barrancas National Cemetery affords another glimpse of the past. Heavily shaded grounds offer beautiful contrast to the sun-drenched white grave markers that are perfectly aligned in every direction. It is quite impossible to pass by this cemetery where the grounds are so inviting and serene without stopping to bide some time.

Just a short distance away is the Pensacola Naval Aviation Museum. Visitors can actually sit in some of the aircraft training modules employed by the Navy to train pilots. The museum, which is free of charge, traces the

Aircraft carrier U.S.S. Enterprise *entering Pensacola Harbor.*

history of flight right up to the Skylab module and offers such attractions as flight simulators and tours by retired aviators. An adjoining I-Max Theatre shows aviation films of unbelievable realism on the big screen. This is also home base to the Blue Angels acrobatic flying team, and schedules of their appearances can be obtained at the base and numerous travel information locations around the city.

There are numerous golf courses in the Pensacola area and include the following:

- Tiger Point Country Club, 1255 Country Club Road, Gulf Breeze; (850) 932–1333, (800) 477–4833

- The Club at Hidden Creek, 3070 PGA Boulevard, Navarre; (850) 939–4604

- Creekside Golf Club, 555 Esperanto Drive, Pensacola; (850) 944–7969

- Marcus Pointe Golf Club, 2500 Oak Pointe Golf Club, Pensacola; (850) 484–9770, (800) 3–MARCUS

- Osceola Golf Club, 300 Tonawanda Drive, Pensacola; (850) 453–7599

- Scenic Hills Country Club, 8891 Burning Tree Road, Pensacola; (850) 476–0611, (800) 477–4833

■ Lost Key Golf Club, 625 Lost Key Drive, Perdido Key; (850)
492–1300, (888) 2–LOSTKEY

The Zoo in Pensacola is home to 700 animals and lush botanical gardens. Veteran's Memorial Park features a replica of the Vietnam Veteran's Memorial in Washington, D.C. Also of interest is the Pensacola Historic Village in Seville Quarter. Call the Pensacola Visitor Information Center at (800) 874–1234 or (850) 434–1234 for more details, or visit their Web site at www.visitpensacola.com.

PHOTO TIPS: Light levels will be extremely low inside the fort, even on a sunny day, so you'll probably need a flash, and a tripod will also be a good idea. Interesting compositions can be obtained looking down the length of the rifle galleries; using a wide-angle lens will be a bonus. Outside on the parade ground, a wide-angle lens will also take in the cannon, flagpole, and other points of interest. Do not overlook the Water Battery on the waterside of the fort. It features some interesting Spanish architectural details that will produce great photos.

Advanced Redoubt 5

The name Redoubt comes from a French word meaning "a protected place of refuge or defense." The word aptly describes the second fort located on the grounds of the Pensacola Naval Air Station.

Here is a fort designed with a specific purpose in mind. Built in the same era as Pickens, McRee, and Barrancas, it was unique in early American coastal forts in that it was intended to repel land-based attacks. Great care was exercised to locate the fort in just the right location for protecting Fort Barrancas and the Naval Yard from an assault from the rear. The structure is trapezoidal in shape and laid out symmetrically around an east-west axis as dictated by the terrain. The ramparts mounted eight large guns. The design was well conceived to make an assault by foot soldiers as costly as possible.

Like Barrancas, the Redoubt has a dry moat with a drawbridge to the entrance, but in this case the moat completely surrounds the fort. A "french drain" was built into the floor of this moat to carry rainwater outside the walls. Please take care not to step into it while strolling about the fort. Both the main walls of the fort (the scarp) and the outer walls of the moat (the counterscarp) feature rifle ports that would cause attackers who entered the moat to be trapped in a deadly crossfire. At the corners of the moat are large portals that have been closed with brick. These embrasures mounted howitzer cannon that could fire buckshot down through the length of the moat.

If the attacking forces did make it to the sally port, the main entrance, howitzer cannon trained on the location would annihilate them with a shower of buckshot. To mount a successful attack against the Redoubt

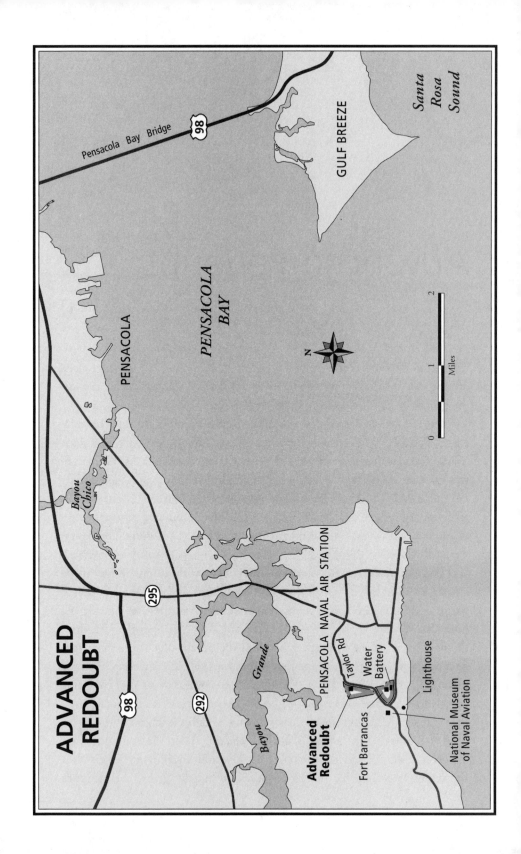

Fort exterior, Advanced Redoubt, Pensacola Naval Air Station.

would have required sacrificing soldiers at a rate faster than the defenders could manage to kill them.

Considered impregnable at the time, the fort was never manned by more than a minimal garrison of soldiers, and in later years would be used as a storage and munitions depot. Today the fort stands very much as it was originally. Years of vandalism and deterioration have taken their toll, and except for repairing the drawbridge mechanism, it has never been restored; therefore, it is not generally open to the public unless escorted by the park rangers. Visitors can, however, walk about the exterior at will, observing the marvelous craftsmanship, which rivals that of Pickens and Barrancas. Benches have been provided on the southern side of the perimeter. Here visitors can rest beneath the marvelous live oak trees and contemplate the insanity of war.

During spring and summer months the NPS offers guided tours of the Advanced Redoubt on Saturdays at 10:00 A.M. Contact the Fort Barrancas Visitor Center (850–455–5167) for more information. A guided tour is well worth the effort if your time allows.

■ Touring the Fort

The ranger-guided tour enters the counterscarp at the rear or western wall and circles around the southern wall, then follows the underground passage across the front wall. One of the first features you'll examine is the embrasure where a cannon once looked down through the moat. The weapon was mounted on a carriage inside the wall and created considerable smoke and enough noise to deafen the operator who ignited it.

Lighting is minimal inside the walls, and certain areas are quite dark; you will be well advised to carry your own flashlight along on the tour. A narrow set of well-worn stairs brings you up into the center of the parade ground, which was manually filled with sand during construction. Returning back down the stairs, the tour continues on around the counterscarp to the door where you entered. The rangers are very knowledgeable about their subject and capable of answering any questions about construction details or history of the structure.

Originally the entire area surrounding the fort was denuded of trees and brush to allow clear views in all directions. Now the fort's location is a peaceful meadow on the picturesque grounds of the naval air station, a setting that belies the hideous purpose for which it was designed. Fortunately the Advanced Redoubt was tested only once in battle, during the Civil War, when 200 dismounted Alabama cavalry attacked (October 1863); it still awaits the foreign attackers who never came.

■ Information

ACCESS: From Pensacola take Highway 292 west. Turn left (south) on Highway 295, cross Bayou Grande, and enter the Pensacola Naval Air Station main gate via the far right-hand lane. The guard should wave you on through, but if stopped, simply advise that you are visiting the national seashore facilities and then follow the signs.

BEST TIME TO VISIT: Anytime of year is fine, but please note that during any time of national emergency, admittance may be denied for base security reasons. Because you will not be participating in water sports, spring, winter, or fall are recommended for visiting, as the weather will be more comfortable.

CAMPING AND LODGING: In the Pensacola area, camping is available at the following:

- Mayfair RV Park, 4540 Mobile Highway; (850) 455–8561

- Timberlake RV Park, 2600 West Michigan Avenue; (850) 944–5487

- Farther west on Highway 292 is the Big Lagoon State Recreation Area with camping available. Call (850) 492–1595 for information and reservations.

Lodging is abundant in the Pensacola area with all major hotel and motel chains represented. When making reservations, request the locations closest to the Naval Air Station.

- Days Inn, 7051 Pensacola Boulevard, Pensacola; (850) 476–9090, (800) 325–2525

- Hampton Inn, 2187 Airport Boulevard, Pensacola; (850) 478–1123, (800) HAMPTON

- Holiday Inn, 6501 Pensacola Boulevard, Pensacola; (850) 476–7200, (800) HOLIDAY

- Motel 6, 5829 Pensacola Boulevard, Pensacola; (850) 477–7522, or (800) 466–8356

The central business district offers an excellent assortment of restaurants, shops, and entertainment.

OTHER INFORMATION: While driving on the Pensacola Naval Air Station property, you are under the jurisdiction of federal authorities, so please drive carefully.

A Web site is available at www.nps.gov/guis/ with more information to help plan your visit.

NEARBY POINTS OF INTEREST: Located just south of Advanced Redoubt is Fort Barrancas, another Gulf Islands National Seashore unit (see previous chapter).

National Museum of Naval Aviation.

Only a short drive away is the Pensacola Lighthouse built in 1825 at a cost of $6,000 and still used today as a navigation aid. The Fresnel lens was created in Paris and is still in use, although the light has been automated and no attendant is required.

The Barrancas National Cemetery affords another glimpse of the past. Heavily shaded grounds offer beautiful contrast to the symmetry of the sun-drenched white grave markers that are perfectly aligned in every direction. So inviting and serene are the grounds that you will surely want to stop and spend some time.

Just a short distance away is the National Museum of Naval Aviation. Visitors can actually sit in some of the display aircraft trainers. The free museum traces the history of flight right up to the Skylab module and offers such attractions as flight simulators and tours by retired aviators. An adjoining I-Max Theatre shows aviation films of unbelievable realism on the big screen.

This base is also home to the Blue Angels acrobatic flying team, and schedules of their appearances can be obtained at the base and numerous locations around the city.

Pensacola Lighthouse.

The Zoo in Pensacola is home to 700 animals and lush botanical gardens. Call (850) 932–2229 for information.

There are many golf courses located in the area:

- Tiger Point Country Club, 1255 Country Club Road, Gulf Breeze; (850) 932–1333, (800) 477–4833

- The Club at Hidden Creek, 3070 PGA Boulevard, Gulf Breeze; (850) 939–4604

- Creekside Golf Club, 555 Esperanto Drive, Pensacola; (850) 944–7969

- Marcus Pointe Golf Club, 2500 Oak Pointe Golf Club, Pensacola; (850) 484–9770, (800) 3–MARCUS

- Osceola Golf Club, 300 Tonawanda Drive, Pensacola; (850) 453–7599

- Scenic Hills Country Club, 8891 Burning Tree Road, Pensacola; (850) 476–0611, (800) 477–4833

- Lost Key Golf Club, 625 Lost Key Drive, Perdido Key; (850) 492–1300, (888) 2–LOSTKEY

Veteran's Memorial Park features a replica of the Vietnam Veteran's Memorial in Washington, D.C. Call the Pensacola Visitor Information Center at (800) 874–1234 or (850) 434–1234 for more details, or visit their Web site at www.visitpensacola.com.

PHOTO TIPS: If you visit only the outside of the fort, you should have sufficient light for all photography. Inside the structures walls it will be quite dark and a flash will be necessary for practically all photography. Architecturally, the structure affords many angles, shapes, and lines that provide intriguing compositions. The interplay of light and shadow on the brick surfaces will also benefit your images.

Perdido Key

Perdido Key is separated from the mainland by Big Lagoon, which became part of the Intracoastal Waterway many years ago. The island has experienced high-density development in both residential and resort properties, and very little open beach remains, accounting for the popularity of the Johnson Beach complex at this unit of the Gulf Islands National Seashore; it has the only public access for miles. Dr. Stephen Leatherman of the Florida International University, who is known as "Doctor Beach," ranked Perdido Key at fifteenth on his 1999 "Best Beaches" list.

At Johnson Beach boardwalks provide access to the whitest sand to be found in Florida and are intended for foot traffic only. They are closed to bikes, skateboards, and in-line skates. Ample parking is provided for those sun worshippers who wish to see and be seen on the beach.

When swimming on the ocean side of the island, be aware of rip tides and currents, especially where children are concerned. The currents can gradually sweep even the strongest of adult swimmers into trouble at times. Caution should also be exercised as the water may contain jellyfish, sea nettle, and Portuguese man-of-war. They have stinging tentacles and can definitely ruin your day. If you suddenly find yourself in a school of small fish, a predator, which may be a much larger fish, is probably pursuing them, and you are well advised to leave the water immediately. Never swim while thunderstorms are in progress—Florida has the highest incidence of lightning of all the states. Pavilions are provided so that you can seek shelter onshore. Swimming is also allowed on the Big Lagoon side of the island and may be safer for small children.

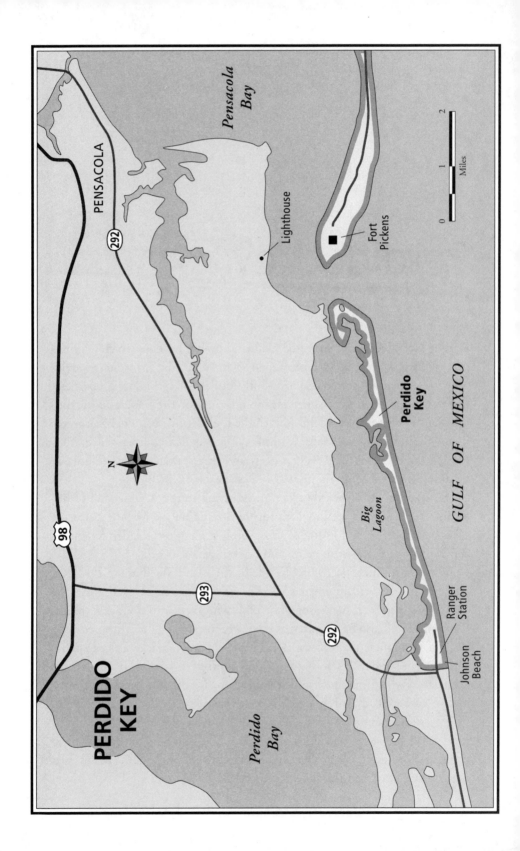

The main road also provides access to a boat launch area capable of handling only small boats. From the beach area the road extends another 2 miles out along the island. Parking is allowed for beach access, but be careful of the loose sand transported by the constant wind. It is quite easy to become stuck along the edges of the pavement.

Here the island is no more than several hundred yards wide, and the environment is all rolling dunes covered in sea oats. In fall and winter flocks of red-winged blackbirds often visit to feed on the seeds of the sea oats, and kestrels soar overhead in search of prey. This is the only known habitat of the extremely rare Perdido Key beach mouse whose populations are declining, possibly due to loss of habitat. Only one hundred or so still exist. For this reason the NPS requests that visitors stay off the dunes, and fences have been erected to protect some critical habitat areas. The creature is mostly white with brown coloration along its back and is a federally listed endangered species. To protect its habitat the NPS is considering closing at least part of the road, which has upset some visitors and many local residents who do not understand the critter's role in this environment.

The beach mouse is an important part of a symbiotic relationship with the sea oats and dunes. As the mouse feeds on the seeds of the sea oat plant, he stores them at his den and various other caches on the island, and the spread of the plant is assured. This relationship grows ever more imperative as continuously increasing numbers of humans flock to the park. In short, for the island to survive, it needs the dunes, the dunes need the sea oats, which need the beach mice! More importantly the mice also serve as a barometer of the environment, according to Michael Wooten, professor of zoology at Auburn University and noted authority on the subject. "Once the mouse starts to disappear, that is a very strong signal that something is awry in the habitat. It is no longer the type of habitat that will support birds, flowers, and other components of the ecosystem." There is an old adage that says, "everything in nature has its purpose," and it is most appropriate at Perdido Key.

Shore birds and sea turtles nest here, and numerous species of birds have been identified on the island. Their presence varies according to the time of year. Threatened nesting birds, such as least terns and snowy plovers, which were driven out of other more heavily developed areas in southern Florida, now frequent these beaches. Pardon the pun, but this may be their last resort! You may also see sanderlings running briskly along the shore, searching for food.

The island continues for approximately 5 miles past the end of the road, to the ruins of some satellite gun emplacements. Battery Slemmer, completed in 1899, mounted two 8-inch breech-loading rifles. Battery Center (1900) mounted four 15-pounder rapid-fire guns, and Battery 233 (1943) was identical to Battery 234 on Santa Rosa Island. Little remains of them today.

The tip of the island was once the location of Fort McRee, which was built in the same era as Forts Barrancas and Pickens. The idea was to trap enemy ships between the three forts in a deadly triangulation of cannon fire. There is nothing left of McRee to see today, but it is mentioned here because it was an important part of this triad of coastal defenses and figured prominently in the Civil War action at Pensacola.

The fort was named for Major William McRee, who served in the War of 1812, and was appointed to the Board of Engineers in 1816, helping to complete the first ever survey for seacoast defenses. Construction of the triple-tiered fort began in 1834 and was besieged with problems from the beginning. Government funding was slow and sporadic in coming, delaying construction on numerous occasions. McRee was virtually completed by the end of 1838, but it had no guns in place until 1845. Meanwhile water leakage caused deterioration of floor timbers that finally had to be strengthened to support the upper tiers of cannon. Engineers fought a constant battle to keep the surf from undermining the fort and the adjacent battery that was added later. Storms from the Gulf occasionally washed over the island, and one created a lagoon behind the fort, effectively separating it from the remainder of the island, then known as Foster's Bank.

The fort only saw action during the Civil War when occupied by Confederate troops—as was Fort Barrancas. When the federally held Fort Pickens, on Santa Rosa Island, and two federal ships shelled Fort McRee almost into oblivion, rendering it useless, Confederate troops withdrew. Some of the bricks were later used for repairs on the other forts, but the hurricane of 1906 leveled the structure, although some remnants of the fort still remained into the 1930s. Subsequent natural erosion of the island's tip has removed any trace of the structure, and its original location is now believed to be underwater.

In summer the tip of the island is very popular with boaters who come to camp out on the shore. The inland side of the island forms two excellent, sheltered coves: one between Langley Point and Redfish Point and the other at Spanish Point, the tip of the island that is shaped rather like a hook. In 1999, *Boating World* magazine named Perdido Key as one of its one hundred best "fantasy island" destinations for boaters, and this area can be quite crowded. With the crowding comes the problem of pollution, and the NPS requests that boaters do not dump waste water overboard.

Near-shore fishing with live bait is popular at Perdido Key, and April and May are productive months. Redfish, pompano, speckled trout, and bluefish are abundant in these waters. Local bait shops can tell you what is being caught at the time of your visit and recommend tackle that you will need.

Please do not litter when camping on the island—and carry away anything you bring with you. Fires are permitted while camping but must be built below the high-tide line on the shore, and you must be more than 0.5 mile beyond the end of the road. Be sure you have adequate drinking water and appropriate sun protection as sunstroke and heat exhaustion are very real threats in summer.

If you do not have a boat, the 5-mile walk to the tip of the island over the loose sand can be quite taxing, and the return trip is even worse. The park service does not recommend it except for the most physically fit of visitors.

■ The Nature Trail

Adjacent to the boat launch is the beginning of a very interesting nature trail that extends inland through a low-rise forest canopy of slash pine and longleaf pine. The undergrowth is a significant community of yaupon holly, gallberry, and wax myrtle that can be a bird-watcher's paradise in fall and winter when these plants produce berries. The yaupon holly will be heavily laden with beautiful bright red berries. The leaves of this plant were once boiled by Native Americans to create a potent brew used to test the mettle of male tribe members. Such information is provided on trailside exhibits,

Jellyfish swimming, Pensacola.

and a small, elevated observation platform overlooks a marshland alongside Big Lagoon.

As the trail continues inland, the environment changes abruptly, becoming a secondary dune community, characterized by dwarf live oak trees, scrub oaks, and Florida rosemary bushes. Here the trail becomes a boardwalk and extends to the main road. While enjoying your stroll, please remain on the boardwalk to protect the fragile dunes.

■ Information

ACCESS: From Pensacola proceed west on Highway 292, which will be named Pace Boulevard, changing to Barrancas Avenue, and finally to Gulf Beach Highway, but always numbered 292. Cross over the Intracoastal Waterway Bridge, which has such an abrupt rise high into the air that it just might take your breath away. At the next curve to the right, turn immediately to the *left* onto Johnson Beach Road and proceed to the entrance gate.

BEST TIME TO VISIT: Summer finds this small beach area quite crowded with tourists and locals, as well. Any other season of the year will be much more enjoyable, but not as warm for swimming or sunbathing.

CAMPING AND LODGING: The closest camping is at the Big Lagoon State Recreation Area back across the waterway, north of the park. Call (850) 492–1595 for information and directions or inquire at the entrance gate.

There are numerous hotels and motels east and west of the park, offering any level of amenities that you may require.

■ Best Western Inn, 13585 Perdido Key Drive, Peridido Key; (850) 492–2755, (800) 554–8879

■ Perdido Sun Condominiums, 13753 Perdido Key Drive, Peridido Key; (850) 492–2390, (800) 227–2390; Web site: www.perdidosun.com

■ Vista Del Mar Condominium, 13333 Johnson Beach Road, Perdido Key; (850) 492–0211, (800) 648–4529

For more information call the Perdido Key Chamber of Commerce, (800) 328–0107 or (850) 492–4660.

OTHER INFORMATION: The day-use area is open daily from 8:00 A.M. to sunset, and all facilities are wheelchair accessible. Johnson Beach features picnic shelters, which are available on a first-come, first-served basis, and rest rooms that are open year-round. A store concession operates only from Memorial Day through Labor Day, and a small ranger station is located at the complex. This is a fee area, and your seven-day pass from any of the other units will be accepted.

Boat rental is available from the Perdido Key Marina, River Road; (850) 492–4944.

NEARBY POINTS OF INTEREST: Big Lagoon State Recreation Area is located nearby on the northern shore of the Intracoastal, and it's worth a visit for its wetland boardwalk, which crosses a typical Florida marsh area. One can view such denizens of the marsh as great blue herons, great egrets, and black-crowned night herons, a nocturnal feeder, among an environment of cordgrass and salt grass on the shallow shoals. The outer end of the walkway rises to an overlook of the Big Lagoon itself. Picnic facilities and a campground with bathhouses are also on the grounds. This park is part of Florida's excellent state park system and an informative brochure, *Florida State Parks: The Real Florida* can be obtained by calling (850) 488–9872, or check the Web site at www.dep.state.fl.us/parks.

PHOTO TIPS: All that beautiful white sand underfoot will fool your camera meter into underexposing your images, so it will be necessary to set the exposure compensation device for from one to one and one-half stops more exposure (overexposure), but only when you see a viewfinder full of white. Use your flash unit when photographing human faces on the beach to eliminate dark shadows around eye sockets or under the rim of a hat. Most new cameras will compensate automatically and correct for the red-eye syndrome.

When not in use protect your photographic equipment from the blowing sand and the hot sun of summer by placing it in a beach bag. High temperatures are especially hard on color films, causing unusual shifts in the color balance.

Special precautions are in order in any beach environment, and this one is no exception. Fine particles of sand floating on the wind are deadly to the inner workings of your electronic camera and accessories. If you must open the camera back (to change film) or change lenses on the beach, do so under a towel or inside a beach bag. Clean your lens frequently with a very soft brush. Do not wipe with a cloth as you might scratch the glass.

Mississippi District

As with the Florida District facilities, the story of the Mississippi District is rich in natural and cultural history. The district administers four barrier islands that lie 10 to 12 miles off the mainland coast near Biloxi. These sheltering islands create the vast Mississippi Sound approximately 80 miles in length, which is very shallow, averaging ten to twelve feet deep, except for shipping channels that are dredged to more than thirty feet. Currents rushing in and out of the sound at tidal changes created Ship Island Pass, the only natural channel. It determined the location of the port of Gulfport when it was established at the turn of the twentieth century. The Biloxi and Gulfport waterfronts on the mainland is an engineered beach of dredged sand, which was created because of the low wave energy and lack of natural sand supply there. Except in the case of storm conditions, there is no surf to speak of, and the only conditions conducive to wave-oriented sports, such as surfboarding or bodysurfing, are found on the south beach of the barrier islands.

Several rivers, including the Pascagoula and Biloxi, dump voluminous amounts of muddy, fresh water into the sound, creating a brackish estuarine environment quite different from the Gulf side of the islands. The barrier islands create a low-salinity, high-nutrient habitat in the sound. The bottom composition is mostly mud with very little sand, and the difference is readily apparent in the dull brown color of the water. This mud composition keeps out most snails, mussels, and clams because it clogs their gills. But the situation changes radically in the waters nearer to the barrier islands where extensive sea grass beds are formed, a rich habitat that supports several hundred species of marine life. Found here are more than twenty species of clams and twenty-five species of crabs, including blue crabs and shrimp, which are the staples of the seafood industry in the area. Compared to other marine communities, sea grass beds are among the most productive in the world, and these owe their existence to the barrier islands. The sea grass beds combine with the vast marshes and estuaries that serve as nurseries to produce a richly varied population of fish for commercial and sport fishing.

In addition to the natural features, the state has created thirty-five artificial reefs as feeding sites for red snapper, speckled trout, cobia, and other species, and maps of these sites can be found at local bait shops. Outside the islands in deep Gulf waters are gas and oil rigs that provide opportunities for trophy amberjack and king mackerel around them. Combine all this with a climate that accommodates year-round fishing, and you have the ingredients for an exciting saltwater fishing experience.

The state of Mississippi does have separate freshwater and saltwater fishing licenses, which can be purchased annually or in three-day increments. Some exemptions are available for age and certain disabilities, so check with the Mississippi Department of Wildlife, Fisheries, and Parks.

There are over thirty public boat ramps in the area, in addition to numerous private fishing camps with ramps and a thriving charter boat industry. The Mississippi Charter Boat Captains Association is an active group whose members are inspected and licensed by the U.S. Coast Guard and includes a variety of boats to accommodate any size party. A free directory of members can be ordered by calling (800) 237–9493 or checking the Web site at www.gulfcoast.org/mgccvb/fishing.htm.

Several fishing tournaments are held annually. They include the Kingmaster 100 in May with a top prize of $50,000, the Gulf Coast Billfish Classic in June, and the Mississippi Deep Sea Fishing Rodeo—the largest event of it's kind—on the Fourth of July weekend. The rodeo has just celebrated its fiftieth year. (Call the 800 number listed earlier for more details and entry forms.)

Davis Bayou

The Colmer Visitor Center at Davis Bayou should be your first stop at the Mississippi facilities. It is located at the end of a tree-shaded lane that winds along the side of the bayou. Four hundred acres are set aside in this park as woods, salt marsh, picnic areas, boardwalks, and nature trails. The grounds are well kept, and guided walks to and along the bayou are provided. Situated behind the building is an elevated observation platform overlooking the water.

The visitor center was named for a Pascagoula congressman, William M. Colmer, who was instrumental in establishing the national seashore. Visitors may pick up informational pamphlets for the various seashore areas and the self-guiding "Nature's Way Trail" at the information desk. Park personnel can provide information you need before visiting the barrier islands and advise about any closed locations. An auditorium provides orientation films on request to familiarize visitors with the great variety of attractions available in the Mississippi District. The major exhibit includes intriguing examples of the paintings of local artist Walter Anderson, whose twenty-year obsession with Horn Island is detailed elsewhere in this book. There are also woodcarvings by John Segeren to illustrate the major seashore habitats of bayous, bays, the sound, the islands, and open Gulf. A historic time line exhibit of Ship Island, a hurricane and weather exhibit, plus the Ocean Springs Art Association quarterly show are all located in the gallery.

The Mississippi District hosts one of the largest Earth Day ceremonies in the state every April. Its elaborate celebration attracts more than 3,000

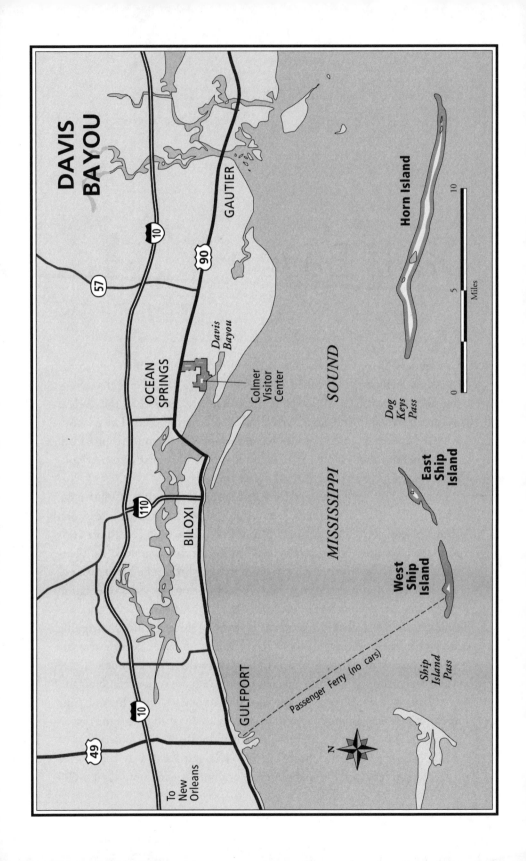

Immature alligator sunning, Davis Bayou.

visitors. It is a family event with many nature-related, hands-on activities for children; exhibitors come from all over the Mississippi Coast. Other activities are organized throughout the year, and schedules are posted at key locations about the park. The International Beach Clean-Up Day is observed the third Saturday of September, and the "Reach for the Beach" clean-up is scheduled the first Saturday of May. Volunteers are welcome at both, and boat captains are always needed to transfer volunteers to the islands. (If you would like to help, phone 228–875–9057 for details.)

Davis Bayou is a tidal marsh environment with water levels that fluctuate according to high and low tides. The elevation varies only a matter of inches in the patchwork of lagoons, but that is enough to support varied plant communities. Part of the bayou will be virtually dry with the tide out, and this is the time when wading birds flock to the mud flats to feed. There may be herons and egrets wading the shallows among the salt grass as kingfishers hover above, prepared to dive headlong into the water after unsuspecting prey. Migrating waterfowl include the stunning hooded merganser, among others; it is a bird-watcher's delight.

Reptiles common to the bayou include snakes, lizards, and alligators that may be seen sunning beside the water's edge. Marsh rabbits peer out from cover in hopes the alligator's morning feeding time has passed. The cycles of life continue here as they have for eons in close association with the whims of Mother Nature.

A 0.5-mile looped nature trail, Nature's Way Trail, starts at the road to the campground. Markers along the way relate to a printed guide available at the visitor center. Elevation along the short trail varies from only three to fifteen feet, but it provides a striking contrast in the plant communities. An observation point allows visitors to view the marsh habitat: The wide, green grasses are spartina, and the darker rounded blades are black needlerush. Both provide nursery habitat for shrimp, blue crabs, and other organisms. If you hear a cluck, cluck, cluck coming from the marsh, it is the clapper rail, a bird that lives its entire life in the marsh.

Checkpoints all along the walk offer a close look at various types of indigenous plant life, including palmetto, beauty berry, sweetgum, yaupon holly, and loblolly pines. At location 15 on the trail is an unusual young tree called the devil's walking stick. Its spiny bark and compound leaf design identifies it as a form of ginseng. Muscadine grapevines and southern magnolia trees with their huge white blooms are other native plants that will be found along your nature walk. Be sure to check out the alligator pond just across the road from the trailhead. Maternal alligators use this blackwater pool area for nesting, and young 'gators can often be seen sunning along the banks.

The Live Oaks Bicycle Route is a 15.5-mile round-trip route between the Davis Bayou area and the Old Train Depot in downtown Ocean Springs. Points of interest along the way include the lovely grounds of the Gulf Coast Research Laboratory, Shearwater Pottery, the Fort Maurepas location, Walter Anderson Art Museum, and the city's Historic District.

The older, original village area of the city of Ocean Springs is quite lovely and quaint and should be included on your itinerary. It is basically a one street town, Washington Street, which is lined with magnificent live oak trees several hundred years old. Highway 90, in the Ocean Springs area, is a typical no-personality American thoroughfare with shopping centers, fast-food franchises, and bumper-to-bumper traffic scurrying about like ants in a disturbed hill; it could be anywhere in the country. But turn south 1 block off Highway 90 on Washington Street, and you enter a different domain where a more relaxed atmosphere is evident. Picture a drug store in business in the same location since 1926, full-service gas stations, and a candy store where New Orleans-style pralines are made fresh daily. Take a walking tour of the village and be reminded of how the 1950s looked.

The city's history dates back some 300 years to the first French settlement on the Gulf Coast area and is closely linked to the history of the barrier islands. French explorer Pierre Le Moyne d'Iberville established Fort Maurepas in 1699, and Ship Island was his base of operations as he explored the area. He chose the location of the fort for the many springs in the area that supplied potable water. The settlement would later be known as Biloxi, Old Biloxi, Vieux Biloxi, and Lynchburg Springs before a New Orleans' physician established a sanitarium to take advantage of the healing waters and coined the name Ocean Springs.

Because of its natural resources, the community would find itself inextricably tied to the sea. As steamboats plied the waters between the ports of Pensacola and New Orleans, Ocean Springs became a regular stop to stock up on wood and water for their boilers. Even when the railroad replaced the steamboats as the preferred method of commercial shipping, the L&N locomotives sought out the same supplies at this wayside village. Ocean Springs has always been home to many of the local fishermen, and later it became the base of operations for the Gulf Coast Research Laboratory, which is today a center for teaching and marine research.

■ Live Oaks Bicycle Route

If you have bicycles, a brochure is available at the chamber of commerce that will route you along a fascinating tour beginning at the Old Train Depot. Chamber personnel can also direct you to local merchants where rental bikes are available.

Here are some points of interest along the way.

■ The Old L&N Depot was constructed in 1907 and was used daily until service was terminated in 1965. The structure was added to the National Register of Historic Places in 1979. Be sure to obtain a brochure from the chamber office detailing the shops of the downtown area, which is your next stop.

■ Proceed south on Washington Street along the lovely tree-shaded street and notice all the interesting shops along the way, including the Candy Cottage and the Lovelace Drug Store that has been in operation since 1926.

■ Next along Washington is the Walter Anderson Museum that was completed in 1991. The museum is open from 10:00 A.M. to 5:00 P.M., Monday through Saturday, and 1:00 to 5:00 P.M. on Sunday. Featured are Anderson's watercolors and drawings from the area, one the boats he used on his Horn Island trips, and the community center where he painted his now famous mural.

■ Turn right on Calhoun Street and enter the Historic District, an area of homes and churches built during the mid- to late nineteenth-century that features some excellent examples of Gulf Coast architecture and those stunning live oak trees.

■ The bike route winds through the streets of the district and eventually deposits you on Beach Drive and along the area known as "Front Beach"—the waterfront.

■ The old Fort Maurepas location, the original French settlement in the area, is on Beach Drive, and the Fort Maurepas Nature Preserve is next door. From here the bike route winds back in toward town and crosses Inner Harbor, where many of the locally owned fishing boats are docked, then continues onto Shearwater Drive.

■ This stop is the Shearwater Pottery Company, the family business of Peter Anderson, Walter Anderson's brother, which has produced pottery from local clay since 1928. Located on the family compound of twenty-five lovely, wooded acres, along the bay shoreline, there is a showroom and family residences in addition to the work area. Hours are 9:00 A.M. to 5:30 P.M., Monday through Saturday, and 1:00 to 5:30 P.M., Sunday afternoon. You may wish to return here later in your automobile for some shopping.

■ Shearwater Drive becomes East Beach Drive and leads along the water's edge to the lovely grounds of the Gulf Coast Research Laboratory, which was founded in 1947 and continues today as a teaching and research facility. If it is true that "location is everything" then this facility certainly scored a big one. If the gate is open, ride in and admire it!

■ From here travel along Halstead Road and Hanley Road to Davis Bayou. The halfway point is at the Colmer Visitor Center. Then return back along East Beach and the route takes you through some lovely residential area, across Inner Harbor again, at a different point, and finally back to the starting point at the old depot.

■ Information

ACCESS: Take exit 57 off I–10, turn south on Highway 57, then west on Highway 90, approximately 4 miles to the entrance of the national seashore on the left, then just follow the signs to 3500 Park Road.

BEST TIME TO VISIT: Depending on your interests, go any time of year. Summer can be quite uncomfortable due to heat, humidity, and insects, but it is best for the beach on West Ship Island. For fishing or exploring the wilderness islands, spring or fall is recommended.

CAMPING AND LODGING: The Davis Bayou Campground near the visitor center has fifty-one spaces with utilities and a tent area. It is most heavily visited during January, February, and March, and no reservations are accepted. It has a large, shaded picnic area with several covered pavilions for groups. They can be reserved by calling the office at (228) 875–9057. A paved boat launch with docks is located at Halstead Bayou, and a minimal fee is charged for its use.

Other camping facilities include the KOA Campground, 7501 Highway 57; (228) 875–2100; and the Bluff Creek Campground, Potican Bayou Road; (228) 826–3958.

There is abundant lodging along U.S. Highway 90 in Biloxi, Gulfport, and Ocean Springs with any level of amenities you may require.

■ Best Western Inn, 1726 Beach Boulevard, Biloxi; (228) 432–0487

■ Comfort Inn, 1648 Beach Boulevard, Biloxi; (228) 432–1993

■ Days Inn, 2046 Beach Boulevard, Biloxi; (228) 385–1155

■ Economy Inn, 1716 Beach Boulevard, Biloxi; (228) 374–8888

■ Holiday Inn Express, 7304 Washington Avenue, Ocean Springs; (228) 875–7555

■ Sleep Inn, 7412 Tucker Road, Ocean Springs; (228) 627–5337

OTHER INFORMATION: There are no entry fees for any of the units of the Mississippi District at the time of this writing. All wildlife and plant life on parklands is federally protected. Do not attempt to feed wild animals, it endangers both you and the animals. They are not pets! There is no beach at Davis Bayou, and swimming in the bayou is not recommended. There are alligators! The NPS has a Web site at www.nps.gov/guis for more details to help plan your trip.

Ranger-led programs are presented weekly throughout the year. Popular summer programs include "Junior Ranger Programs" for children ages six through twelve and "Sea Star Programs" for children three through five. Activity schedules are located at the visitor center front desk.

A private support group of volunteers exists here, and new members are welcome. Contact them at the following address:

Friends of Gulf Islands National Seashore
P.O. Box 1734
Gulfport, MS 39502

NEARBY POINTS OF INTEREST: A host of events take place in the area year-round, including two events on the must-see list: the Fort Maurepas Living History Weekend in mid-October and the Peter Anderson Arts and Crafts Festival on the first weekend of November. This latter event has been chosen by the Southeastern Tourism Society as one of its top twenty events. Call (228) 875–4424 for more details or check the Web site at www. oceanspringschamber.com.

The Walter Anderson Museum, where you can learn the entire story of the man and his art, is worth a visit. It is located at 510 Washington Avenue, Ocean Springs; (228) 872-3164.

■ Shearwater Pottery, the Anderson Family's pottery business since 1928, is located at 102 Shearwater Drive and the showroom is open daily. Call (228) 875–7320 for information.

- Beauvoir, the home of Jefferson Davis, is at 2244 Beach Boulevard, Biloxi; (228) 388–9074.

- Visit the Scott Marine Aquarium, an excellent family experience, at 115 Beach Boulevard, Biloxi; (228) 374–5550.

Gambling is legal in "resort areas" of Mississippi and the Gulf Coast area is home to numerous casinos located along U.S. 90 near the water in Biloxi. Look for the outrageous decor, you cannot miss them!

- Grand Casino, 265 Beach Boulevard, Biloxi; (228) 436–2946, (800) 946–2946

- Isle of Capri, 151 Beach Boulevard, Biloxi; (228) 435–5400, (800) THE–ISLE

- Presidents Casino, 2110 Beach Boulevard, Biloxi; (228) 385–3500, (800) THE–PRES

- Grand Casino, 3215 West Beach Boulevard, Gulfport; (228) 870–7777, (800) 946–7777

Numerous activities take place on the Mississippi Gulf Coast during the year and a partial list follows:

- Mardi Gras Festivities, January

- Annual Spring Pilgrimage, April

- Cobia Tournament, May

- Deep Sea Fishing Rodeo, June

- Gulf Coast Billfish Classic, June

- Biloxi Seafood Festival, September

Actual dates vary each year, for details contact the Mississippi Gulf Coast Convention and Visitors Bureau at (800) 237–9493 or check the Web site: www.gulfcoast.org

Golf is prevalent in the area and facilities include the following:

- Blackjack Bay Golf Links, 15312 Dismuke Drive, Biloxi; (228) 392–0400

- Dogwood Hills Golf Course, 17476 Dogwood Hills Drive, Biloxi; (228) 392–9805; Web site: www.dogwoodhills.com

- Edgewater Bay Golf Club, 2674 Pass Road, Biloxi; (228) 388–9670

- President Broadwater Golf Club, 200 Beauvoir Road, Biloxi; (228) 385–4081, (800) 843–7737; Web site: www.presidentbroadwater.com

- Great Southern Golf Club, 2000 East Beach Boulevard, Gulfport; (228) 896–3536

- Pine Bayou Golf Course, 5200 CBC 2nd Street, Gulfport; (228) 871–2494

- Windance Country Club, 19385 Champion Circle, Gulfport; (228) 832–4871

- Gulf Hills Golf Club, 13701 Paso Road, Ocean Springs; (228) 875–9663; Web site: www.gulfhillsgolf.com

- St. Andrews Golf Club, 2 Golfing Green Drive, Ocean Springs; (228) 875–7730, (800) 875–7730; Web site: www.golfinggreen.com

PHOTO TIPS: A telephoto lens of 200–300 mm is best for good photos of the wildlife. If you do not own one, check your local camera stores for availability of rental equipment. When using the bigger lenses, you will need to shoot at higher shutter speeds in the range of 1/250 or 1/500—even higher when photographing from a boat. This may require using a higher speed film than you typically use with your normal lens.

Ship Islands
and Fort Massachusetts

Lying approximately 10 miles off the coast of Mississippi are East and West Ship Islands. Prior to 1969 they were one. Camille, the most horrendous of hurricanes to make landfall on this coast, sliced the island into two parts, and the passage between is now known as Camille Cut. In 1991 the National Park Service estimated West Ship at 555 acres in size and East Ship at 362 acres, figures that are subject to change over the years. Twice before this island had been severed by storms and subsequently repaired itself. Only the future will indicate if this will occur again.

The year 1969 was the most active hurricane season on record at the U.S. Weather Service, and no storm since has equaled the wrath of Camille. It roared ashore on the mainland at Biloxi, Mississippi, as a Category 5 storm with sustained winds of over 175 mph, and gusts to 206 mph. The storm surge was an awesome wall of water twenty-five feet high! The devastation was complete; longtime residents had difficulty finding their way around because there were no landmarks left. Camille left more than 250 dead in its wake, and Ship Island was changed—perhaps forever.

The tenuous nature of these islands is perhaps best demonstrated by history. This chain of islands once included Dog Key, located between Ship and Horn Islands, a paradise of sand dunes, flowering oleander, and gently swaying sea oats. Dog Key can still be found on early maps of the area, but it no longer exists, and its story is quite fascinating.

In 1925 two developer/promoters purchased Dog Key at a price of $1.25 per acre with the intention of building a resort. Local Indian legends

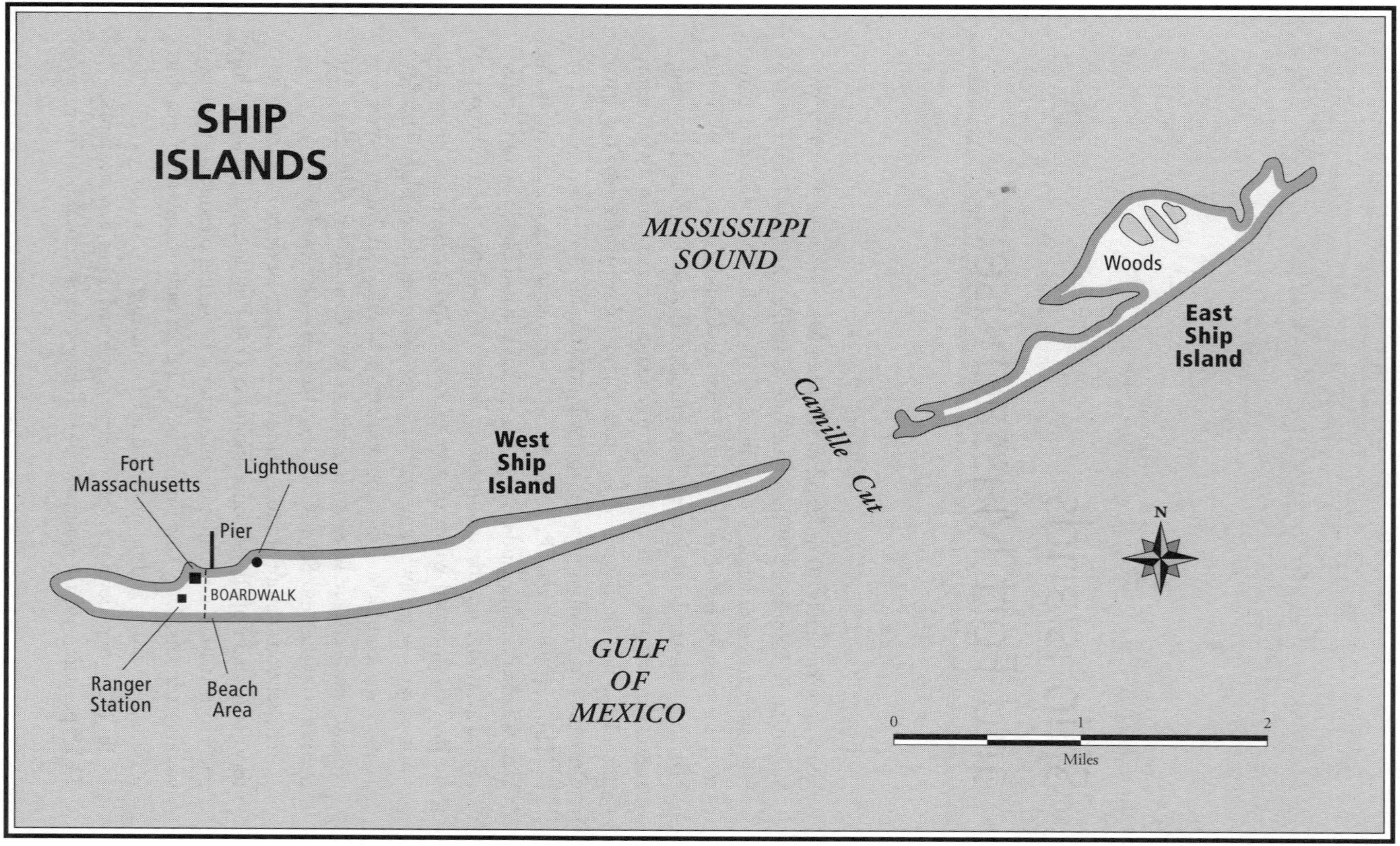

SHIP ISLANDS

East Ship Island

Woods

West Ship Island

MISSISSIPPI SOUND

Camille Cut

GULF OF MEXICO

Lighthouse

Pier

Fort Massachusetts

BOARDWALK

Beach Area

Ranger Station

N

0   1   2

Miles

Fort Massachusetts, West Ship Island.

dating back centuries told of the island's periodic disappearance, and experienced sea captains warned against the venture. Against all best advice, the promoters constructed a raised pavilion to house a casino, dance hall, restaurant, and bathhouses. Cabanas for overnight guests were connected by boardwalks, and electricity was provided by a gasoline generator.

The name Dog Key did not quite project the image the owners wanted, and it was changed to Isle of Caprice. Promotional events included fishing tournaments, swimming marathons, and beauty contests. Gambling took the form of roulette wheels, dice tables, and card games. The north side of the island was dredged for construction of a 1,000-foot pier. Three converted schooners transported guests to the island, and when business prospered, a fourth boat was added. Stage and screen star Ethel Barrymore even visited during the resort's heyday, but by 1930 this booming business was in trouble.

It was noticed that when storms lashed the island, the water never receded properly, and serious erosion of the dunes, which had been stripped of their sea oats, was in progress. By mid-summer of 1931, the island was almost totally awash, and a "mysterious fire" broke out during the fall season, leaving the complex in ruin. By the summer of 1932, the sea had reclaimed the entire island, and it has never resurrected itself. Was this simply a matter of human folly? Definitely, but it was also a barrier island doing what comes naturally, and it now exists only as a shallow shoal. The current barrier islands of the national seashore are more stable, but they are still subject to the whims of nature. See them while you can—they are open to visitation, and West Ship Island is an excellent place to begin.

Throughout its history West Ship Island has been the subject of much human development and offers most of the amenities of a mainland beach. For those who are not interested in the total isolation of wilderness, but still wish to experience the barrier islands, West Ship will be idyllic. Numerous activities are available, enough to fill the day for the entire family: fishing, swimming, beach walking, shell collecting, birding, and ranger-led tours of Fort Massachusetts, a fine example of a third system of coastal forts.

Tour boats provide transportation to the island beginning in March and continuing through the summer season, and the one-hour boat ride is an experience in itself (see "Access"). A flock of laughing gulls follows the boat out to the island and back. Watch closely, and you will likely see dolphins cavorting in the Mississippi Sound. The rest of the year you will need a private or chartered boat to reach the island. The regular ferry service is, perhaps, the reason West Ship Island has greater visitation each year than the other islands, approximately 100,000 people annually. Many of the locals take the ferry out to the island solely to go fishing. The long boat dock is a favorite place to catch small sharks that are cruising the sea grass beds.

Near the boat dock on the north side of the island are picnic pavilions, a ranger station with rest rooms and a first-aid station, and Fort Massachusetts. A boardwalk crosses the island to the oceanside shore, a distance of only 0.3 mile, leading visitors to a beach with bathhouse and showers, snack bar, and a beach store with chair and umbrella rentals. Ship Island is the only one of the islands with any food service available.

As you cross the boardwalk, notice the terrain on both sides. It is a typical barrier island interior swale—a shallow wetland. Wildflowers bloom along the edges, and aquatic plants that exist in the life-giving moisture provide sustenance for migrating waterfowl. You may see wading birds in search of small fish among the salt grass. It is a fascinating look at one facet of barrier island composition.

Visitors can find a taste of the undeveloped island on the eastern end, but the only way to reach it is on foot. The island is 3 miles long, and beach strollers should be cognizant of the time as tour boat operators will not wait for stragglers. Summer temperatures will usually be in the nineties with high humidity; the possibility of sunstroke is ever present. The NPS recommends drinking plenty of water, using a strong sunscreen, and wearing a good hat.

For an additional charge the ferry will take you to East Ship Island. Although it does not have official wilderness designation, the island is totally natural and wooded, and camping is allowed anytime of year. Moving between East and West Ship Islands, it is possible to see the shoals where Hurricane Camille severed the island. The shallower water is lighter in color and very striking. Some visitors seek shells here, but it is dangerous because the depth fluctuates with the tides, and you may be caught off guard.

Ship Island appears in very early historic accounts of Gulf exploration. It was first sighted by one of Pierre Le Moyne d'Iberville's men in 1699, and the French named it Isle aux Vaisseaux. Because of the protective harbor, d'Iberville used it as a base of operations while exploring the Mississippi River and the Gulf Coast. In 1701 he directed the construction of a magazine and barracks on the site and then a fort and warehouse in 1717. By 1722 his interest in the settlement at New Orleans caused him to lose interest in Ship Island, and the island lapsed into obscurity.

Ship Island first appeared in U.S. history during the War of 1812 when nearly sixty British ships and approximately ten thousand soldiers used it as a staging point for an attack on New Orleans. Following that war the United States recognized the deepwater harbor at Ship Island Pass as crucial to the defense of the Gulf Coast and authorized construction of a fort to guard it. During the Civil War, Confederate forces occupied the incomplete fort for a short period in 1861 and then relinquished it to Federal forces for the duration. In addition to Fort Massachusetts, some forty other buildings were constructed during the Civil War, and for a time, the complex served as a prison camp for captured Confederate troops. Some never left the island; 153 were interred there in a burial area now believed to be underwater.

In 1880 Ship Island became the first U.S. quarantine site for ships entering the ports of Pensacola and New Orleans. The timing was fortunate as a yellow fever epidemic in 1882 taxed its facilities. Several ships were held here for fumigation, and a number of sailors died in the hospital. Death was very much a part of life on Ship Island.

■ Touring Fort Massachusetts

The centerpiece of this GINS area is the fort, which was built in the mid-nineteenth century to protect the shipping lanes, the Mississippi coastline, and New Orleans from enemy attack. Construction of the facility began in 1859 and lasted for seven years, during which time it was interrupted by inclement weather, pestilence, and the Civil War itself. War caused a shortage of labor and local supplies, and many of the construction materials were shipped from New England. This was one of the last masonry coastal forts constructed, and unlike the mainland forts, more concrete than brick was used in its construction. Still several million brick were employed in the arched casements and passageways that supported the cannon above. The concrete foundations extend more than nine feet below sea level, and the exterior brick walls are as much as eight feet thick. Spiraling granite staircases were employed between floors to save space, and the powder magazines were lined with wood to help keep the powder dry. An oven was constructed in the main courtyard so cannonballs could be heated, as red-hot cannonballs would do more damage to wooden ships.

The shape of the structure is a horseshoe-like semicircle with half bastions at each end of the squared wall to allow cross fire in defense of the front entrance or sally port. Although thirty-seven cannon were planned, only seventeen were ever mounted in the fort, including two 15-inch Rodman guns that were among the largest smoothbore cannon ever manufactured. The barrels weighed 50,000 pounds and fired cannonballs that weighed 400 pounds with a range of approximately 3 miles. Unfortunately most of these cannon were sold for scrap iron in 1901. One has since been restored to the fort.

Fort Massachusetts was constructed overlooking Ship Island Pass, one of the few natural deep-water channels on the Gulf Coast and an important navigation route to and from New Orleans. Like the other forts in the coastal area, this beautifully crafted facility fell victim to advancing military technology. Masonry forts were designed to withstand attack by smooth-bore cannon, but rifled cannon developed during the Civil War were more powerful and accurate and capable of destroying such fortifications, which were rendered useless.

NPS rangers treat visitors to guided tours twice daily, and two videos are shown in one of the powder storage rooms. The intricate passages built into the walls of the fort are excellent for exploration, but visitors are asked to stay off the earthen mounds atop the walls to prevent erosion. The island's lighthouse stands east of the fort, a short stroll away. When you go, walk the water's edge and look for shells and other surprises that wash ashore. But remember that this is a part of the national seashore, and all plants and animals are protected. Only the *uninhabited* shells are collectable.

■ Information

ACCESS: West Ship Island is only accessible by boat. Tour boat operators, Pan Isles, Inc., transports visitors to the island from Gulfport, leaving from a pier next to the Coast Guard station at the intersection of U.S. Highway 90 and Highway 49. The ferry service operates from March through October. Call (228) 864–1014 or (800) 388–3290 for information.

It is possible to visit the island at other times of year if you own a boat. The visitor center has available a list of NPS inspected and approved charter boat operators. Private boat owners should plan their trip carefully, considering the weather and necessary provisions, and should not anchor within 500 feet of the swimming area on the south beach.

BEST TIME TO VISIT: Summer will be best for enjoying the beach facilities. But if you only wish to explore the island and/or the fort, you might consider spring or fall. Transportation may cost more in the off-season but the advantages are fewer insects and less heat, humidity, and tourist crowding. At certain times of year, sections of the undeveloped end of the island may be closed, during bird nesting season, for instance. Please check with the ranger station on the island before entering.

Fort Massachusetts, West Ship Island.

CAMPING AND LODGING: No camping or overnight visitation is allowed on West Ship Island, but it is allowed on East Ship Island, Horn Island, and Petit Bois Island. The following camping facilities are available on the mainland:

- Davis Bayou Campground (an NPS facility) on Hanley Road near the visitor center, with 51 spaces, plus group tenting area; no reservations

- Bluff Creek Campground, Potican Bayou Road, Ocean Springs; (228) 826–3958

- KOA Campground, 7501 Highway 57, Ocean Springs; (228) 875–2100

Numerous lodging facilities are available along the coast in Biloxi and Gulfport, offering any level of amenities you may require. Reservations are recommended.

- Best Western Inn, 1726 Beach Boulevard, Biloxi; (228) 432–0487

- Comfort Inn, 1648 Beach Boulevard, Biloxi; (228) 432–1993

■ Days Inn, 2046 Beach Boulevard, Biloxi; (228) 385–1155

■ Economy Inn, 1716 Beach Boulevard, Biloxi; (228) 374–8888

OTHER INFORMATION: No glass containers are allowed on the islands. If you take them along, you must leave them on the boat. Except for the top level of Fort Massachusetts, all park facilities on West Ship Island are wheelchair accessible. Two beach wheelchairs are available on a first-come, first-served basis.

Pets are not allowed on tour boats or in all buildings on the island, including the fort and picnic shelters. Ranger-led activities, special presentations, and beach programs are posted at the island ranger station.

The use of metal detectors on the island is banned to protect any archaeological, historical, or cultural resources that may still be undiscovered.

When swimming, use caution to avoid jellyfish and stingrays. Protect yourself at all times against insect bites, sunburn, and heat exhaustion. Drink plenty of water.

NEARBY POINTS OF INTEREST: The wilderness islands, Horn Island and Petit Bois Island, are only a few miles away and are accessible only by charter boat. (See chaps. 9 and 10 for details.)

On the mainland the Walter Anderson Museum is of interest and depicts the life and art of a man obsessed with these islands. You'll find it at 510 Washington Avenue, Ocean Springs; (228) 872–3164.

Beauvoir, the home of Jefferson Davis, is at 2244 Beach Boulevard, Biloxi; (228) 374–5550. Consider Scott Marine Aquarium, 115 Beach Boulevard, Biloxi; (228) 374–5550.

The Mississippi Sandhill Crane National Wildlife Refuge at 7200 Crane Lane, Gautier, (228) 497–6322, is also worth a visit.

Gambling is legal in resort areas of Mississippi, and the Gulf Coast area is home to numerous casinos located along U.S. Highway 90 near the water. Look for the outrageous decor, you cannot miss them!

■ Grand Casino, 265 Beach Boulevard, Biloxi; (228) 436–2946, (800) 946–2946

■ Isle of Capri, 151 Beach Boulevard, Biloxi; (228) 435–5400, (800) THE–ISLE

■ Presidents Casino, 2110 Beach Boulevard, Biloxi; (228) 385–3500, (800) THE–PRES

■ Grand Casino, 3215 West Beach Boulevard,Gulfport; (228) 870–7777, (800) 946–7777

Numerous activities take place on the Mississippi Gulf Coast during the year and a partial list follows:

■ Mardi Gras Festivities, January

■ Annual Spring Pilgrimage, April

■ Cobia Tournament, May

■ Deep Sea Fishing Rodeo, June

■ Gulf Coast Billfish Classic, June

■ Biloxi Seafood Festival, September

Actual dates for these events vary each year, for details contact the Mississippi Gulf Coast Convention and Visitors Bureau at (800) 237–9493 or visit the Web site at www.gulfcoast.org.

PHOTO TIPS: Insect repellant is all important when visiting the barrier islands, and when you apply it to your skin, be sure to wipe your hands before handling your camera. The deet contained in most of these preparations is harmful to the polycarbonate cases used by most camera manufacturers. And because these repellants are petroleum-based solutions, keep them off your lenses as well.

Pay attention to your exposures when shooting on the white sand beaches, or you may have underexposed images. Some compensation is required when you see a lot of white in your viewfinder, and your camera manual should outline procedures for such situations. Always take extraordinary precautions in any beach environment to protect your camera from airborne sand particles.

Horn Island

Horn Island is approximately 14 miles long and is estimated at 3,535 acres by the National Park Service. It features the most varied terrain of the two wilderness islands and the best hiking. Cross trails are maintained at either end of the island; crossing near the center, where the island is 1 mile wide, is possible at a trail near the old chimney, the only one on the island. Otherwise crossing at the island's center can be difficult due to a dense patchwork of vegetation, pine forests, and numerous lagoons. Ponds on the island include Long Pond on the east tip, Garden and Water's Pond, and Middle Ponds. Two others, Big Lagoon and Ranger Pond, have openings to the Mississippi Sound and, therefore, a more brackish water content. Smaller ponds, sometimes found near the water's edge, are called cat-eye ponds and occur when shifting sands close off a small indention in the shoreline.

The island has more than 470 acres of maritime forest, primarily live oaks and slash pine, some as old as ninety-one years. The majority of the live oaks are located along the north side of the eastern tip of the island. Some very large trees are buried by sand dunes as much as twenty feet high, leaving only the trees' upper branches exposed, which take root and spread.

Various stickers and cactus spines, and the fact that summer heat makes the sand hot enough to burn bare feet, makes shoes a necessity when hiking here. One of the more interesting plants you might observe is the dodder, a vine that grows over other trees and bushes. It derives its energy from the host plant, and because it is not involved in photosynthesis, it does not

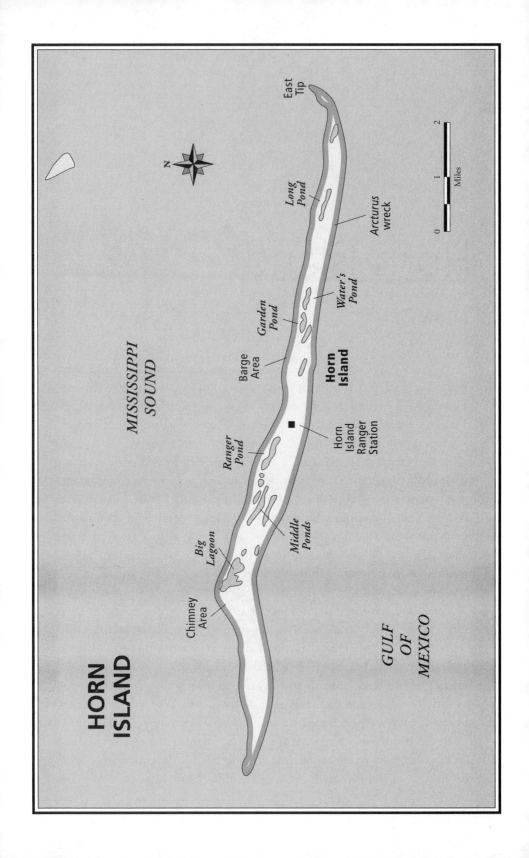

Great blue heron takes flight, Horn Island.

produce chlorophyll—its color will be a yellow-orange all year-round. Conradina, a low-growing shrub with delicate lavender blooms, is also found on the island and is indigenous only to this area of the Gulf.

These islands have been the subjects of considerable scientific study. More than 250 species of birds have been identified in the islands, and some nest here. Plovers and sandpipers probe the shore for food, including seaworms, sand fleas, and larvae. Sanderlings stop off to rest and feed during their 8,000-mile journey between the Arctic and South America. Peregrine falcons, hummingbirds, and numerous species of warblers visit during spring and fall migrations. This is the first landfall for many northbound spring migrants that have crossed the Gulf from the Yucatan Peninsula or the northern coast of South America. Many will make it, some will not. Often they starve to death on the wing and fall dead into the water; others will land on the islands too exhausted to survive. During the long flight some species use up all their fat reserves and even use some muscle proteins as a supplemental source of energy. They arrive in the barrier islands fat free and dehydrated and stay to replenish and recuperate.

Neotropical bird migrations begin in February with purple martins, and by mid-March significant flights of passerines arrive. In early April the probability of favorable weather over the Gulf increases, and until mid-May flights are constant, as indicated by radar observations, except for when strong cold fronts are located over the southern Gulf.

Huge sea turtles occasionally scoop out nests on the beach to lay their eggs, and alligators may be seen sunning by a pond. Few mammals occupy this island, but raccoons, otters, rabbits, and nutria—somewhat similar in appearance—may be seen. The nutria is an exotic, originally from South America. They were imported into Louisiana for farming purposes but were known to roam wild in the area. The U.S. Fish and Wildlife Service believes they came to the island during one of the numerous hurricanes. NPS personnel consider them a nuisance because the animals feed on the rhizomes of sea oats, which are so important to stabilizing the island's sand. The nutria is fuzzy like a muskrat, but it has a small round tail without hair. Raccoons, on the other hand, have a bandit mask on a whitish face and a fuzzy tail with rings of black and light yellow. Swamp rabbits have a similar brown fur on their body, but they have rust colored fur on feet and face, and their habitat is marshes and bottomland. These adorable creatures evade predators by entering water and swimming alligator style with only eyes and nose visible.

Just offshore the water teems with shrimp, squid, horseshoe crabs, and jellyfish, and surf fishing is quite popular. These waters also are famous for mullet, speckled trout, flounder, and Spanish mackerel. No permit is necessary from the NPS, but a state saltwater license is required. You should also be aware of Mississippi State fishing laws and restrictions on gill netting and the taking of shrimp, oysters, and female blue crabs.

A ranger station is located on Horn Island, approximately at the middle, and the resident ranger is responsible for administration of both wilderness islands. The officer has the option to close various parts of the island during wildlife nesting season. The station is a private residence and not open to the public.

Horn has the most coastline of the islands and is the better location for shell collection; if you arrange to be there at low tide, you will be more successful. The Florida horse conch is the largest of all U.S. mollusks and has been made scarce by collectors. It is more likely found while diving or snorkeling. Florida and alphabet cones will be found along the oceanside shore-line, and the latter is the most colorful. They have venom that is used to capture prey, and although it is not considered deadly to humans, if the shell is occupied, please handle it carefully and return it to the water. The comb bittersweet, common nutmeg, and Florida lucina are common in the islands along with smaller items like coquinas and ceriths. Following a winter storm you may find most anything washed up on the beach.

Gulf Coast hurricanes occasionally produce natural phenomenon called hurricane balls. They are round or egg-shaped balls, varying in size, and constructed of tightly woven plant materials around a central core object that may be as small as a cigarette butt or as large as a soda pop can. The balls may contain many forms of organic matter, including pine straw, palmetto fibers, and spartina marsh grass, which appears to be a basic ingredient. Only the larger storms produce hurricane balls, and after Camille ravaged the Gulf Coast in 1969, over one hundred balls were found on the beaches of Horn Island alone. More than 1,500 were found in the Biloxi area. After much study scientists believe the balls are a product of the mechanical motion of water within the waves created by the storm. Only the surface of the wave moves any distance. Individual particles of water within move in orbitals (circles), weaving the reeds together. When the wave reaches water where the depth is twice the height of the wave, the circular materials are forced upward, forming the egg-shaped balls. Camille was an extraordinary storm and produced hurricane balls that were exceptional in both size and number.

History is as apparent in these islands as minute grains of sand. Many of the world's great powers have left their "imprints" here. Arrowheads and pottery fragments found on the island indicate that its first visitors were aboriginals, coastal Indians who came for the abundant food. These may have included the Biloxi, Pascagoula, and Capinan tribes that traversed the sound in canoes made of hollowed-out cypress trees. Ship's logs of the French explorer Bienville indicate that he spotted Indians on the beaches of Ship Island in 1699 when he claimed the islands for his country and gave them names. During the sixteenth and seventeenth centuries, pirates used the islands to prey upon Spanish galleons laden with gold in the Gulf of Mexico. Oral history accounts indicate several colonial families lived on Horn for brief periods from 1700 to 1900. The Waters family moved there in 1845, and they and succeeding generations raised livestock for 75 years. The U.S. Army took over Horn Island during World War II and left its mark. A biological warfare experiment station was established and included a short section of narrow gauge railroad. The facilities were abandoned in 1945 and lost to a hurricane in 1947.

In more recent years the island has been littered with the detritus of seamen. About 1 mile east of the ranger station on the north shore are the remains of old sunken barges, which are visible most of the time, depending on the tides. East of the ranger station on the south coast is the remains of a wrecked crew boat, the *Arcturus*, that sits right on the beach. All of these are rusting hulks and unsafe for exploration.

Each of these groups defiled the wilderness islands as humans are wont to do, but fortunately little remains of their influence as Nature has slowly reclaimed the island.

■ The Island Experience

Thoreau would be proud! When he wrote, "In wilderness is the preservation of the world," it was a very insightful statement considering the time, for he could not have known what modern life would be like in the twenty-first century. Each day brings ever-increasing demands on our time, and that situation can only worsen.

Many humans have an inherent desire to escape occasionally from the humdrum city life, to commune with nature, to refresh the spirit. For those who seek isolation from the rigors of their daily lives, for those who have ever dreamed of being on a desert island, no place could be better than the wilderness islands of the Gulf Islands National Seashore. To step onto one of these islands is to step back in time to a world seemingly untouched by the hand of humankind. It is a sensory experience: the sight of untamed animals living in the wild, the sound of water lapping at the shore, the smell and taste of the ocean breeze on the tongue. So complete is the isolation that it is possible to take a solitary walk along a secluded beach without meeting another person, and it is difficult to believe that just a few short miles away is the bustling Mississippi Coast. These islands are more than physically separated from the mainland; they are spiritually separated as well. There is an enduring quality here, a feeling that the Earth has always been like this. But in reality barrier islands are some of the Earth's youngest geologic events; some created as recently as 3,000 years ago.

Ephemeral as they are—totally subject to the action of wind, waves, and currents—these islands have long captured the imagination of humans. Artist Walter Anderson, of Ocean Springs, Mississippi, was such a man, and no account of Horn Island would be complete without his story.

During his lifelong career as a painter, potter, writer, and wood-carver, Anderson developed an obsession with Horn Island, the largest of the wilderness islands. He worked primarily in watercolors and drawings and amassed a tremendous body of work, some of which he destroyed in his darker moments. Many of his paintings were unknown even to members of his own family until after his death. In the cottage where he worked, the family found a chest filled with some two thousand paintings and water-colors, only a fraction of his work, many on the subject of his beloved island.

Walter was also a prodigious author and wrote at length about his island experiences. Some of Anderson's island logs have survived and tell of a man totally in touch with his senses. He spoke of light and color, of poetry and music. It was obvious that he was truly alive only when walking the shores of Horn Island.

Born in New Orleans in 1903, the second son of a Scottish grain merchant, he was educated at St. John's School, in Manlius, New York, until the age of fourteen when he returned to New Orleans. Later he would study at the Parson's Institute in New York, then the Pennsylvania Academy of Fine Arts in Philadelphia where he became preoccupied with such masters of drawing as Degas, Ingres, and Dürer. In 1925 he won the Packard Award for animal draw-ing in a student competition, thus setting the stage for his life's work.

At the end of his studies in Philadelphia, in 1928, Walter traveled to France where he was disappointed in the art schools and studios of Paris. He set about an exploration of the French countryside on foot and bicycle and was taken with the cave paintings of Dordogne. When he returned to America, his family had moved to Ocean Springs, Mississippi, and estab-lished a pottery business.

Walter met and, in 1933, married Agnes Grinstead while struggling to establish a career in art. He worked part-time in the family business and

Brown pelican, endangered, Horn Island.

accepted commissions to supplement his income. In 1935 he painted a historical panorama in the auditorium of the Ocean Springs High School. Later he painted a mural in the local community center, which survives today as a part of the gallery that honors his work. In his personal art the works of Adolpho Best-Maugard and Jay Hambridge inspired him, and their influences can be found in his drawings of birds, fish, and plant life.

As with many artists Walter's work was not appreciated during his lifetime. Even while creating the community center mural, he had to endure the jeering and criticism of local residents. Anderson withdrew into himself. In an area known for its eccentricity, he gained a reputation as a recluse, hardly speaking and always shabbily dressed. At 37 Walter spiraled into mental illness. He was in and out of institutions for several years without success; finally he turned to his love of nature as therapy.

For many years, beginning in 1946, he rowed or sailed a ten-foot boat filled with art supplies and food across 12 miles of the Mississippi Sound to the barrier islands, where he lived and worked in primitive conditions. At night he slept on the beach—under his boat in bad weather—and by day studied in detail the island's plant and animal life, sand and marsh, often for weeks at a time. He was sometimes moved to travel on to the Chandeleur Islands, which lay farther to the west, near the coast of southern Louisiana. They were the nesting grounds of the brown pelicans that were dominant in his thoughts and work. Anderson wrote of his trips in daily journals, some of which have been published in book form, *The Horn Island Logs of Walter Inglis Anderson*. Some ninety of these logs still exist and make extremely interesting reading. One recurring thread is woven throughout the journals: Anderson's love of, and fascination with, the brown pelicans that he traveled so far to see. He frequently sketched and painted them in watercolors and observed them at every opportunity. Anderson even came to think he could understand their "language" and wrote his interpretations of how it sounded in his journals.

While the islands today are still shelters for wildlife, the abundance that Walter documented no longer exists—except in his art and words. Following World War II scientists woke up to the fact that DDT pesticides in agricultural runoff were contaminating fish and other prey that pelicans feed on. The same chemical poisoning that drove the bald eagle to the brink of extinction was accumulating in the pelican's tissues, causing them to lay thin-shelled eggs that broke under the weight of the parent birds. Their numbers dwindled, along with many other species, until the use of such pesticides was outlawed and abolished in 1972 by the Environmental Protection Agency. Another great naturalist, Rachel Carson, was largely responsible for calling this tragedy to the public's attention in her landmark book, *Silent Spring,* published in 1962.

Almost extinct at the time, the pelicans are slowly making a comeback, but they still face many hazards and are still considered endangered. Pelicans prefer to feed in shallow estuary environments or shoaling shore-lines, such as are found in the barrier islands, where small schooling fish are plentiful. But many coastal areas are polluted with spilled gas and oil that damage pelican feathers and are toxic when ingested. Major spills from ships and drilling rigs have been known to destroy entire populations. Discarded fishing lines and six-pack rings are waste items that account for many deaths, and commercial fishers who consider the birds competition kill them whenever possible. Acid rain is fast becoming a factor, also, as it makes their habitats unlivable.

Pelicans are so well adapted to their environments that they have remained virtually unchanged since prehistoric times, but modern man may finally be the cause of their extinction if more protective measures are not instituted. How sad Walter Anderson would be if he knew of the decline of his beloved birds since his demise.

Wildlife was not his only interest however. From Walter Anderson's log dated September 1959: "I took a long walk yesterday afternoon to the east and drew trees. I like the wandering ones, not absolute freaks but not just the ordinary healthy ones either. There are some wonderfully strange ones on Horn Island—years of storm and years of sudden growth, one side retarded and the other growing like a vine." Walter probably wrote of the live oaks that often grow in grotesque shapes, especially in the harsh environment of the barrier islands. His words and his art even detailed exposed plant root systems that he found interesting. Nothing escaped the scrutiny of his analytical mind.

Walter wanted to become part of nature, to experience every part, even in its most destructive state. When Hurricane Betsy hit New Orleans in 1965, it grazed by Horn Island while Anderson was in residence. Ignoring the Coast Guard, who were asked by his wife to pick him up, Walter found the highest ground, tied himself to a tree, and outlasted the storm, which completely swamped the island in places.

Walter's logs speak of the power and majesty of the storm: "Never has there been a hurricane more respectable—the tide is high and in several places is eating chunks out of the beach." His usual campsite disappeared, sliced away by the raging sea. Anderson moved his camp to higher ground several times, stopping once to sketch three mice. "I left in a hurry intending to recamp on the high dune of Tern Point. When I got there it seemed almost an island already, so I kept on wading, sometimes up to my chest, in and out among the flooded trees—no rain, for which I was very thankful."

Following the storm Walter made two trips to New Orleans for scientific information on it. He consumed newspaper files and other sources and also consulted with meteorologists about this storm with which he felt such a close kinship.

Anderson was so enamoured with his work that he ignored all else, even his family on the mainland, and his obsession lasted until his death from cancer in 1965.

Author John D. McDonald was also intrigued by these islands and was moved to write a novel on the subject, *Barrier Island*. His story is about an unscrupulous real estate speculator who attempts to profit from the sale of an additional island to the National Park Service. According to Gail Bishop, Chief Interpretive Officer at GINS, McDonald's story was loosely based on actual events surrounding the government's acquisition of a barrier island in Mississippi. Coincidentally, at the time of this writing, the NPS is negotiating to purchase part of Cat Island as an addition to the park and to protect it from development.

Although somewhat demeaned by human habitation and abuse, Horn Island is almost as enchanting today as it was in Anderson's day. It can still be an exciting experience for visitors. When you visit, leave all that left brain stuff behind at the office or at home. Take the photography or painting gear along and exercise the right brain for a change. Get in touch with your creative side as you experience these extraordinary islands!

■ Information

ACCESS: Access to the wilderness islands is by private or chartered boat only. If you travel by private boat, plan carefully, attending to weather, provisions, water, and fuel. None of these are available on the island.

The visitor center at Davis Bayou has available a constantly updated list of inspected and approved charter boat operators that provide service all year and can land passengers at the NPS dock on the island. Please call (228) 875–0074 for details.

BEST TIME TO VISIT: Depending on your interests, go anytime of year. Summer is best for swimming, but it can be quite uncomfortable due to heat, humidity, and insects. For exploring the island spring or fall is recommended. At certain times of year, sections of the island may be closed to public visitation, during nesting season, for instance. Please check with the visitor center before going.

CAMPING AND LODGING: Overnight wilderness camping is allowed on the island year-round, but there is no formal campground. Information about recommended locations on the island are available from the visitor center. A tent with netting fine enough to stop the minuscule, biting insects called "no-see-ums" is recommended. Insects such as deerflies, mosquitoes, and sand gnats hatch all year and are unpredictable. When they are swarming, camp on the windward side of the island. Fires should be built on the

Great egret and alligator, Horn Island.

shore below the high tide line; no camping is allowed within 300 feet of a tree with a nesting osprey.

On the mainland the Davis Bayou Campground near the visitor center has fifty-one spaces with utilities and a tent area. No reservations are taken. Other campgrounds include:

- Bluff Creek Campground, Potican Bayou Road, Ocean Springs; (228) 826–3958

- KOA Campground, 7501 Highway 57, Ocean Springs; (228) 875–2100

There is abundant lodging along U.S. Highway 90 in Biloxi and Gulfport with any level of amenities you may require.

- Best Western Inn, 1726 Beach Boulevard, Biloxi; (228) 432–0487

- Comfort Inn, 1648 Beach Boulevard, Biloxi; (228) 432–1993

- Days Inn, 2046 Beach Boulevard, Biloxi; (228) 385–1155

- Economy Inn, 1716 Beach Boulevard, Biloxi; (228) 374–8888

- Holiday Inn Express, 7304 Washington Avenue, Ocean Springs; (228) 875–7555

■ Sleep Inn, 7412 Tucker Road, Ocean Springs; (228) 627–5337

OTHER INFORMATION: A few words about self-preservation: *Take responsibility for your own safety!* Be advised that if you are in trouble on a wilderness island, a call to 911 on your cell phone will not bring immediate assistance. A cell phone is a poor substitute for good common sense and sound judgment when you are 12 miles out to sea.

Plan carefully, considering weather, fuel requirements, water and food needs, and check with park rangers before departing. Be certain that someone on the mainland knows where you are! The ranger station on Horn Island has other full-time responsibilities and is not there to help visitors who get in trouble because of their own negligence. All wildlife and plant life on the islands is federally protected. Do not attempt to feed wild animals, it endangers both you and the animals. They are not pets! There are considerable fines for picking wild plants in the park, please don't do it. The use of metal detectors on the island is banned to protect any archaeological, historical, or cultural resources that may still be undiscovered.

NEARBY POINTS OF INTEREST: Petit Bois Island lies to the east and is half the size of Horn. Although not formally designated as wilderness, the eastern part of Ship Island is undeveloped and makes good exploring. Both are accessible only by private or charter boats.

Davis Bayou at the visitor center is an interesting tour, and the Walter Anderson Museum, where you can learn the entire story of the man and his art, is also worth a visit. It's at 510 Washington Avenue, Ocean Springs; (228) 872–3164.

■ Other places worth considering include:

■ Beauvoir, the home of Jefferson Davis, 2244 Beach Boulevard, Biloxi; (228) 388–9074

■ Scott Marine Aquarium, 115 Beach Boulevard, Biloxi; (228) 374–5550.

■ Mississippi Sandhill Crane National Wildlife Refuge, 7200 Crane Lane, Gautier; (228) 497–6322.

Gambling is legal in resort areas of Mississippi, and the Gulf Coast area is home to numerous casinos located along U.S. Highway 90 near the water. Look for the outrageous decor, you cannot miss them!

■ Grand Casino, 265 Beach Boulevard, Biloxi; (228) 436–2946, (800) 946–2946

■ Isle of Capri, 151 Beach Boulevard, Biloxi; (228) 435–5400, (800) THE–ISLE

■ Presidents Casino, 2110 Beach Boulevard, Biloxi; (228) 385–3500, (800) THE–PRES

■ Grand Casino, 3215 West Beach Boulevard, Gulfport; (228) 870–7777, (800) 946–7777

Numerous activities take place on the Mississippi Gulf Coast during the year and a partial list follows:

■ Mardi Gras Festivities, January

■ Annual Spring Pilgrimage, April

■ Cobia Tournament, May

■ Deep Sea Fishing Rodeo, June

■ Gulf Coast Billfish Classic, June

■ Biloxi Seafood Festival, September

Actual dates vary each year, for details contact the Mississippi Gulf Coast Convention and Visitors Bureau at (800) 237–9493 or check its Web site: www.gulfcoast.org

PHOTO TIPS: Take care to protect your equipment from sand and salt spray, especially on the boat ride. As with all beach shooting at the Gulf Islands National Seashore, you will need exposure compensation for scenes that include a lot of very white sand. Check your camera manual for instructions. Long focal length lenses are recommended for wildlife photos and can be rented from dealers in the area before you go to the islands. Please do not approach wild animals too closely, attempting to use your normal lens. Light will be plentiful, except in the worst of weather, and any film you prefer should suffice.

Petit Bois Island

10

Early French explorers named all of these barrier islands as they explored the Gulf Coast in search of suitable colonization locations. Pierre Le Moyne d'Iberville claimed the area for France in 1699, a claim that would not survive with so many nations seeking colonies in the New World. Ship Island was called Isle aux Vasseaux originally for its natural harbor, Horn Island was named Isle a Come for a powder horn lost there, and Petit Bois was named for its small wooded section. The last is the only French name that would endure over the centuries, and the locals now pronounce it like "petty boy."

The island is far smaller than Horn Island, approximately 6 miles in length and 1,466 acres. It's primarily barren except for a small area of brackish and freshwater marshes and trees—only about fourteen acres of woods—at the eastern end. Petit Bois has not experienced fire in over twenty years so shrubs dominate the interior. Forest development comes slowly to these islands: First the dunes must be stabilized by sea oats, salt grass, and pennywort; further inland may be prickly pear, palmetto, and eventually live oak. Slash pines manage to take hold and reproduce. Violent storms that periodically rake the area interfere with this gradual process, and then there is always the destructive hand of humans, so the "little woods" have remained exactly that.

Barrier islands are a paradox: We humans tend to think of a land mass as something permanent, but the natural creative forces at work here are so delicate that any impact from humans or the elements can threaten their existence. Many centuries ago Petit Bois was a part of Dauphin Island,

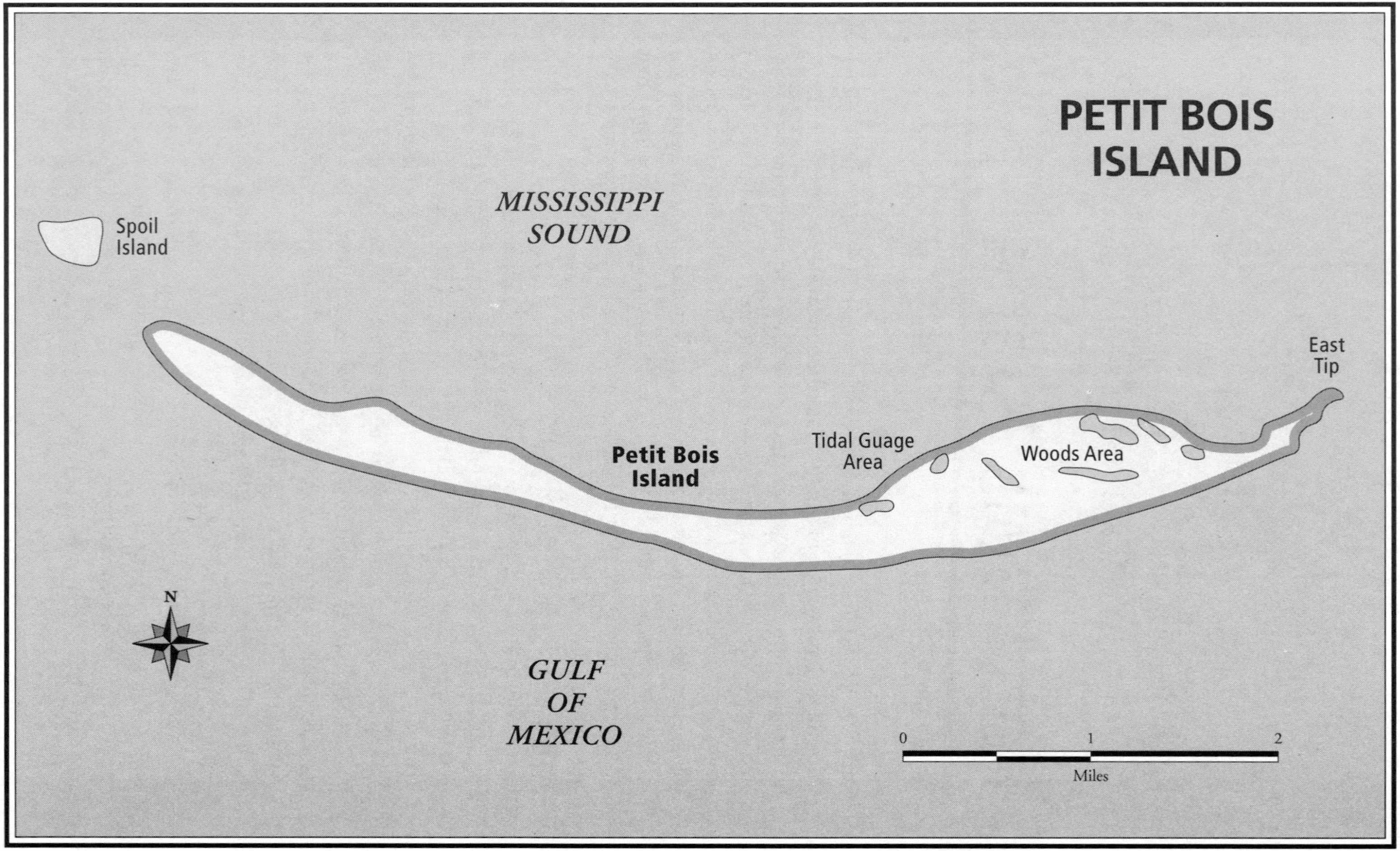

PETIT BOIS
ISLAND

East
Tip

Woods Area

Tidal Guage
Area

Petit Bois
Island

Spoil
Island

MISSISSIPPI
SOUND

GULF
OF
MEXICO

N

0   1   2
Miles

located off the coast of Alabama. A rogue hurricane sliced off the western tip, and it has since drifted to the west to become the island we know today.

The NPS manages the wilderness islands for maximum protection of wildlife. Petit Bois and Horn Islands are important habitat and nesting grounds for waterfowl, such as terns, herons, and egrets. Blue geese, snow geese, and loons winter here, along with many species of ducks, and the island comes alive with migrating songbirds in spring. This is the first landfall for many species on their northward migration across the Gulf. In October and November the island will be peppered with monarch butterflies, also on their migration route. The inland ponds are home to alligators, and snakes are frequent visitors in the almost unbearable heat of summer, so approach with caution. As you explore the island, keep your eye on the Gulf waters. The islands are good locations for dolphin watching, and you may see them surface on either side of Petit Bois—the sound side as well as the ocean. As with the other islands, sport fishing is allowed in the waters surrounding the island. A Mississippi saltwater fishing license is required.

There is no development of any kind on the island, no ranger station, no comfort station, so plan accordingly if you intend to camp on the island. If you visit in summer, expect ninety-degree-plus temperatures and very little shade. There is also very little protection from a storm. Biting insects can be a problem, so use repellent and plan to camp on the windward side of the island. Cutting trees on the island is not allowed, even the dead trees that serve as nesting locations for wildlife, so you may want to carry some firewood. Otherwise please limit your fires to the driftwood you can find on the beach and burn campfires only below the high tide line. Plan carefully, considering weather, fuel requirements, and water and food needs and check with park rangers before departing. Be certain that someone on the mainland knows where you are! The park ranger from Horn Island patrols by boat but cannot share fuel or supplies with you.

■ The Island Experience

Prepare yourself for enchantment! The first time you cross the Mississippi Sound in summer and see this island materialize on the shimmering horizon, you will wonder why you waited so long for such an experience. It is truly an adventure. From the air the island appears as a small splotch of white on a vast palette of blue and green, with accents provided by the whitecaps of waves on the shallow shoals. The feeling is primeval, as if you have been deposited on an oasis, the only spit of land in this vast Gulf.

Some visitors may find Petit Bois's solitude a bit overwhelming, especially those accustomed to city life. But total isolation may just be the crux of the island's charm and attraction, the reason so many people visit every year. The western end of Petit Bois is primarily barren, a sandy peninsula just begging for long strolls at sunset or lounging in the refreshing water. If you swim while visiting the island, be aware that jellyfish are common in these waters in late summer, and stingrays can be found hiding in the sandy bottom. Neither is aggressive, but you and the jellyfish may wander into each other, and if you step on the stingray, it will respond by lashing out with its barbed tail, which can cause swelling and intense pain.

Feel free to collect the shells you find on Petit Bois as long as they are uninhabited. Following high tide you may find such treasures as sea stars and shark's teeth. Lightning whelks are also common on these shores. All just hint at what awaits below if you go snorkeling or scuba diving. When it comes to plant life on the island, the situation is quite different—it should be left in place. Each and every plant, especially the sea oat, is helpful in anchoring the loose sands of this delicate habitat. Please do not disturb any beach-dependent birds you may find nesting, and be aware that the sea turtles that occasionally nest here are protected under the Marine Mammal Protection Act.

Try your hand at surf fishing if so inclined. These waters teem with squid, shrimp, silversides, and other species that attract larger game fish, and you should be quite successful. Mullet, flounder, and speckled trout are found in these waters, and boat owners will want to troll for Spanish mackerel.

■ Information

ACCESS: Access to the wilderness islands is by private or chartered boat only. If you go by private boat, please be aware of the NPS's suggestions for anchoring along the shoreline. These are provided for your own safety and the protection of your craft and are outlined in the camping brochure available at the Davis Bayou Visitor Center.

The visitor center also has available a constantly updated list of inspected and approved charter boat operators who provide service all year and can land passengers on the island. Please call (228) 875–0074 for details.

BEST TIME TO VISIT: Summer is best for swimming but can be quite uncomfortable due to heat, humidity, and insects. For exploring the island spring or fall is recommended. At certain times of year, sections of the island may be closed to visitation, during nesting season, for instance. Please check with the visitor center before going.

CAMPING AND LODGING: Overnight wilderness camping is allowed on the island year-round, but there is no formal campground. Three recommended locations on the island are designated on a map available at the visitor center.

On the mainland the Davis Bayou Campground near the visitor center has fifty-one spaces with utilities and a tent area. No reservations are taken. Also nearby are the Bluff Creek Campground, Potican Bayou Road, Ocean Springs; (228) 826–3958; and the KOA Campground, 7501 Highway 57, Ocean Springs; (228) 875–2100.

There is abundant lodging along U.S. Highway 90 in Biloxi and Gulfport with any level of amenities you may require.

■ Best Western Inn, 1726 Beach Boulevard, Biloxi; (228) 432–0487

■ Comfort Inn, 1648 Beach Boulevard, Biloxi; (228) 432–1993

■ Days Inn, 2046 Beach Boulevard, Biloxi; (228) 385–1155

■ Economy Inn, 1716 Beach Boulevard, Biloxi; (228) 374–8888

OTHER INFORMATION: A few words about self-preservation: *Take responsibility for your own safety!* Be advised that if you are in trouble on a wilderness island, a call to 911 on your cell phone will not bring immediate assistance. A cell phone is a poor substitute for good common sense and sound judgment when you are 12 miles out at sea. The Coast Guard in the area monitors VHF channel 16 for emergencies.

All wildlife and plant life on the islands are federally protected. Do not attempt to feed wild animals; it endangers both you and the animals. They are not pets. There are significant fines for picking wild plants in the park, please don't do it!

The use of metal detectors on the island is banned to protect any archaeological, historical, or cultural resources that may still be undiscovered.

If you suffer a stingray "attack," soaking the wound in hot water for thirty minutes can produce some relief from the pain. Seek medical attention as soon as possible because a tetanus shot may be required.

NEARBY POINTS OF INTEREST: Horn Island is next door and more than twice the size of Petit Bois. Although not formally designated as wilderness, the eastern part of Ship Island is undeveloped. Both are accessible only by private boats.

There is an interesting tour of Davis Bayou, starting at the visitor center. The Walter Anderson Museum at 510 Washington Avenue, Ocean Springs; (228) 872–3164 is also worth a visit.

You might also enjoy Mississippi Sandhill Crane National Wildlife Refuge, 7200 Crane Lane, Gautier; (228) 497–6322; or Beauvoir, the home of Jefferson Davis, 2244 Beach Boulevard, Biloxi; (228) 388–9074.

Gambling is legal in resort areas of Mississippi, and the Gulf Coast area is home to numerous casinos located along U.S. Highway 90 near the water. Look for the outrageous decor, you cannot miss them!

- Grand Casino, 265 Beach Boulevard, Biloxi; (228) 436–2946, (800) 946–2946

- Isle of Capri, 151 Beach Boulevard, Biloxi; (228) 435–5400, (800) THE–ISLE

- Presidents Casino, 2110 Beach Boulevard, Biloxi; (228) 385–3500, (800) THE–PRES

- Grand Casino, 3215 West Beach Boulevard, Gulfport; (228) 870–7777, (800) 946–7777

Numerous activities take place on the Mississippi Gulf Coast during the year, and a partial list follows:

- Mardi Gras Festivities, January

■ Annual Spring Pilgrimage, April

■ Cobia Tournament, May

■ Deep Sea Fishing Rodeo, June

■ Gulf Coast Billfish Classic, June

■ Biloxi Seafood Festival, September

Actual dates vary each year, for details contact the Mississippi Gulf Coast Convention and Visitors Bureau at (800) 237–9493, or check their Web site: www.gulfcoast.org.

PHOTO TIPS: Take care to protect your equipment from sand and salt spray, which is especially prevalent on this almost barren island. As with all beach shooting at the Gulf Islands National Seashore, you will need exposure compensation for scenes that include a lot of the extremely white sand. Check your camera manual for instructions. Use long focal length lenses for wildlife instead of approaching too closely to use your normal lens. Local camera shops will have such equipment available for rent. Light will be abundant, and lower speed films should suffice, except in the worst of weather conditions.

In Conclusion

C artoon character Pogo once stated: "I have seen the enemy and it is us!" Second only to a major hurricane, human intervention is the most destructive force affecting the barrier islands today.

Development of barrier islands along the East Coast, from New Jersey south to Georgia, has proven over and over the fallacy of such endeavors. In typical American style we try to control the uncontrollable and force these islands to act unnaturally. Historically the Army Corps of Engineers, those proponents of the idea "masters of all we survey," have wasted astronomical sums of tax dollars trying to control sand beaches. The East Coast is littered with their failed attempts.

When permanent structures are erected, the inevitable erosion begins. A good example is the much publicized, and enormously expensive, relocation of the Cape Hatteras Lighthouse on the Outer Banks of North Carolina. Even here in the Gulf Islands National Seashore where the National Park Service is charged with maintaining Fort Massachusetts, which was built on the weakened, shifting sands of Ship Island, it has been necessary to fortify the eroding shoreline with dredged soil to protect the foundation of the structure.

Perhaps wilderness designation is the best that could have happened to protect the islands of the GINS. How fortunate we are that there were visionaries to mount the movement, which brought these islands under a protective umbrella. Like cowboys of the Old West, the islands are free spirits and resist being corralled. By nature they are creatures of change, and when allowed to change, barrier islands can readily provide sanctuary for nature, wildlife, and for people.

Appendix A:
For More Information

National Park Service
Southeastern Region
75 Spring Street Southwest
Atlanta, GA 30303
(404) 331–4998

Florida Parks Information
Mail Station 535
3900 Commonwealth Boulevard
Tallahassee, FL 32399
(850) 488–9872
www.dep.state.fl.us/parks

Florida Historic Sites Information
R. A. Gray Building
500 South Bronough Street
Tallahassee, FL 32301
(850) 487–2333

Florida Bureau of Archeological Research
500 South Bronough Street
Tallahassee, FL 32301
(850) 487–2299

Florida Oceanographic Society
890 Northeast Ocean Boulevard
Stuart, FL 34996
(407) 225–0505

Blackwater River State Park
Route 1, P.O. Box 57-C
Holt, FL 32564
(850) 623–2363
www.dep.state.fl.us/parks

Mississippi Gulf Coast Visitors Bureau
P.O. Box 6128
Gulfport, MS 35906-6128
(800) 237–9493
www.gulfcoast.org

Pensacola Historical Society
117 East Government Street
Pensacola, FL 32501
(850) 434–5455

Saltwater Fishing Information
Department of Environmental Protection
Fisheries Management
Mail Station 240
900 Commonwealth Boulevard
Tallahassee, Fl 32399
(850) 488–7326

Fresh Water Fishing Information
Florida Game and Fish Commission
620 South Meridian Street
Tallahassee, FL 32399
(850) 488–2975
www.state.fl.us/gfc

Florida Native Plant Society
P.O. Box 680008
Orlando FL 32868

Florida Trail Association
P.O. Box 13708
Gainesville, FL 32604
(850) 378–8823

Florida Audubon Society
460 Highway 4
Suite 200
Casselberry, FL 32707
(850) 260–8300

Blackwater Canoe Rental
(800) 967–6789
(850) 623–0235
Fax: (850) 623–3973

Ocean Springs Chamber of Commerce
P.O. Box 187
Ocean Springs, MS 39566
(228) 875–4424
www.oceanspringschamber.com

Mississippi Department of Wildlife, Fisheries, and Parks
1505 Eastover Drive
Jackson, MS 39211
(601) 432–2400
www.mdwfp.com/licensefishing.asp

Appendix B:
Additional Reading

Bartram, Travels and Other Writings
New York: The Library of America, 1984

Confederate Forts
Zed H. Burns
Natchez, Miss.: Southern Historical
Publications, 1977

Ecosystems of Florida
Ronald Myers and John Ewel
Orlando, Fla.: University of Central Florida
Press, 1990

Encyclopedia of Historic Forts
Robert B. Roberts
New York: Macmillan Publishing, 1988

A Field Guide to Shells of the Florida Coast
Jean Andrews
Houston, Tex.: Gulf Publishing Co., 1994

*First Encounters: Spanish Exploration in the
Caribbean and the United States*
Jerald T. Milanich and Susan Milbrath
Gainesville, Fla.: University Presses of
Florida, 1989

Florida Archaeology: An Overview
Florida Anthropological Society
Tampa, Fla.: Florida Anthropological
Society

Florida Parks
Gerald Grow
Tallahasse, Fla.: Longleaf Publications,
1997

Florida Wildflowers and Roadside Plants
C. Ritchie Bell and Bryan J. Taylor
Chapel Hill, N.C.: Laurel Hill Press, 1982

Florida Wildlife Viewing Guide
Susan Cerulean and Ann Morrow
Helena, Mont.: Falcon Publishing, 1998

Florida's Hurricane History
Jay Barnes
Chapel Hill, N.C.: University of North
Carolina Press, 1998

The Hiker's Guide to Florida
Timothy O'Keefe
Helena, Mont.: Falcon Publishing, 1993

*The Horn Island Logs of Walter Inglis
Anderson*
Jackson, Miss.: University Press of
Mississippi, 1985

Islands at the Edge of Time
Gunnar Hansen
New York: Island Press, 1993

The New History of Florida
Michael Gannon
Gainesville, Fla.: University Press of
Florida, 1996

Pensacola: Spaniards to Space-Age
Virginia Parks
Pensacola, Fla.: Pensacola Historical
Society, 1996

Seashell Collectors Handbook & Identifier
Sonya B. Murray
New York: Sterling Publishing

Index